A Difficult Passage

from prairie poverty to heights beyond

Ray Wiseman

WordWise Associates
Fergus

A Difficult Passage

Published by:

WordWise Associates
Fergus, Ontario

Printed in Canada

ISBN: 0-9688917-0-5

Dedicated to Anna who proofreads every line I write.
Although she did not experience the life portrayed
herein, she shares every moment in imagination.

ALSO BY RAY WISEMAN:

I Cannot Dream Less

Aunt Harri Walks the Line

Disciples of Joy

Acknowledgements

Each time I sit down to write, I have the sensation of a crowd of people looking over my shoulder. Although that might sound a little scary, it really is a good thing. I refer to the people who read and comment on my material before it gets anywhere near a printing press. I owe special thanks to the following folks who read and reacted to every page of this book.

- Anna Wiseman, who read every page even more often than I did, applying her special proofreading skills. If you find a typo, I likely caused it by editing something following her last reading!
- Ellen Wheller, who has influenced and contributed to my life since the day I stepped off the train.
- Shirley Wood, who read with the care and concern one would expect from a sister.
- Richard and Merle Vincett. Rich, who appears in the story under an alias, has remained a lifelong friend.
- Nancy Lindquist, who took time to read and comment while in the midst of writing and promoting her own books.
- Donna Mann, who read with her heart, not just her eyes.
- Tena Baker, who tested some of the text by reading it to her husband, Jim.
- Mark Clayton who applied his artistic touch and graphics skills to the cover.
- Pauline Whyte who used similar talents and skills to complete the page layout in readiness for the printer.

And that list doesn't include all my readers and friends who encouraged me to complete this project!

—Ray Wiseman, Fergus, Ontario

Contents

Foreword

They say everyone has a story to tell. Maybe so, but few can tell their story as well as Ray Wiseman. *A Difficult Passage* takes a fascinating look at life through the eyes of a child. The book quickly drew me in, with three things in particular catching my interest. The first is Ray's phenomenal memory of his childhood, which allows him to give us a vivid glimpse of life on the prairies during the depression. The second is the great difference between the boy who was and the man who is—the one so vulnerable and sensitive, the other so confident and at peace. The third is the knowledge that the one became the other not so much in spite of the difficulties of his youth, but because of them. *A Difficult Passage* tells an engaging story of real life, with all its stings and scars, but with humour and liveliness as well, offering hope to all who face struggles.

—N. J. Lindquist, author

Introduction

This story has its genesis in the great migration of people who poured into Canada's western provinces in the early years of the 20th century. They came from England, Scotland, Germany, Scandinavia, Ukraine, and a dozen other places including many States of the Union.

Although the primary account begins with the crystal-clear memories of a two-year-old arriving at the village of Gawain in April of 1936, flashbacks will transport you to earlier times. War in South Africa and Europe, followed by resettlement in a land of promise, shaped the parents who in turn influenced the life of the child—a child who would face a harsh prairie life with its own special terrors and temptations.

We have changed the name of the town and most of the people to protect the innocent—and those who merely think themselves innocent.

Prologue

Fred Stone peered from the window of the gently rocking railway coach as it made its way from Edmonton, through Camrose and on toward Gawain. His athletic, wiry body sat stiffly upright in the seat like an eagle searching for prey from atop a cliff. Few men 40 years younger or a foot taller could match the strength or agility of his five-foot, two-inch frame. People who knew him well, called him Pop.

Pop contemplated the Alberta countryside, not seeing many visible changes since leaving it five years previously to retire in England. Yet he knew depression and terrible dust storms had greatly increased the hardships of prairie farmers. Indeed the long tentacles of depression had reached him in England. When income from the farm at Gawain ceased, he could see no other route but return to the prairie soil and start all over again. He must begin again at age 60 with a young wife, Harriet, and two preschool children, Fred Junior and Stan. Fortunately, he still had the farm —and six dollars in his pocket.

Start over again. He'd been doing that all his life! He leaned back on the seat and closed his eyes, hardly aware of Stan's sleeping body sprawled across his knees. His mind moved back through dim hallways of time to the first occasion when he had started over.

Returning from the Anglo Boer War, he found his wife had abandoned him and their four children. Back in civilian life in England and facing economic hard times, he found it difficult but pulled his life back together. He remarried, returned to life as a shopkeeper, and rejoined his buddies at the cycling club. But two years in South Africa had stirred his imagination. He had visited enough of the world to want to see more. So he made major plans to start over again.

In 1907 they emigrated to Canada to homestead in the newly-formed province of Alberta. After two years apprenticeship with another farmer, he claimed his free land and moved into a tiny sod house with his wife and four kids. In another two years he built a house and outbuildings on the banks of a little valley that intersected his land—westerners call those steep-sided valleys *coulees*.

How often those early days had been a living hell! One day saw him looking over 100 acres of golden wheat—a crop that should produce 50 bushels to the acre. The next day he stood in the same place gazing at the same crop destroyed by hail. For weeks he had spent 12 hours a day preparing the land and putting in that crop. He had fended off black clouds of mosquitos that attacked any exposed flesh and drove the horses to distraction. And now, all for nothing!

Well he would get another chance the next year. But in years that hail didn't get the crops, frost or lack of rain often did.

One winter the snow completely covered the tiny sod house. It took four hours to dig free. In summer they had carried water from a shallow well by a *slough* (rhymes with *shoe*)—a shallow natural pond that held water throughout the year. But when the slough froze solid in winter, they had to melt snow to get water for themselves and the animals.

In later years they had other problems. Dust storms blackened the heavens for hours and appeared intent on moving Alberta's topsoil all the way to Ontario. But he defeated all the setbacks and challenges—he succeeded when many failed.

In the late 1920s Pop tired of farming, passed on to his family or otherwise disposed of all of his land except the original 160-acre homestead and an adjoining 160 acres. Then he prepared to enjoy the fruits of his labours.

He embarked on a year-long world tour, but on return, found nothing to do, so began farming again. By this time people had begun calling him Pop—although he really didn't feel his age. Then his wife died suddenly. With his children grown and gone, he felt lost in an empty house. True to style, he started all over again.

In February 1931, he married Harriet after a whirlwind courtship by mail. Fred Junior arrived in November of that year. The next year Pop and Harriet put the farm into the hands of a daughter and son-in-law and retired to England. Their second son arrived in England.

But now a financial setback and gathering war clouds in Europe had forced him back to Gawain to start over once again. Surely this would be the last time!

The blast of a whistle, the squeak of steel brakes on steel wheels, and the attendant jolt brought Pop out of his reverie and awoke Stan. From their window on the right side of the train they could see Gawain spreading southwest from the tracks. Pop's deep-set, dark eyes sparkled. He loved Gawain. It had little more than a post office when he first came here.

Now about 200 people lived in the village served by an assortment of establishments that included two general stores, a post office, a lumber yard, a John Deere dealership cum hardware, a service station with one pump, a Chinese restaurant, and a hotel with six rooms and a bar. Pop wondered how many businesses had changed hands in five years.

The grain elevators stood to the left of the tracks and not visible from the window. Pop had heard a new company had added a sixth during his time away.

He could easily see two two-story brick buildings standing out against the sketchy skyline—buildings that gave the village its importance in the greater farming community: the Gawain hospital, run by the Sisters of St. Joseph, and the Gawain Consolidated School. He had strongly supported building the bigger central school, even though it meant the removal of the one-room school that had stood on his property.

As the train slowed to walking speed, Pop got a good view of the tiny Mennonite church—his brother-in-law had served as its second pastor. At first it had seemed odd having a Mennonite church when he would have more readily supported the Methodists, but it and a Catholic church had quickly become important parts of the community.

Pop grinned when he noticed someone else taking a keen interest in Gawain. Stan had pressed his nose tightly to the window. As he watched Stan, he reflected, "It's been an exciting life, but a hard life. Dear God, one day let it get easier—it must get easier. If not for me, for my children, for my grandchildren."

Section One: *Gawain*

When I was a child,
    I talked like a child,
        I thought like a child,
            I reasoned like a child. . .

Chapter I

A *new life*

A window on Gawain

I'm Stanley Stone—call me Stan. This is mostly my story, but I've invited you to join me just two months before my third birthday. You just met my dad—I, like everybody else, always called him Pop. Back then, Pop and I got along really well. Mother said that's because I'm the "youngest son of his old age." She also said that Fred Junior, my older brother, "has got his nose out of joint because of it." I didn't have a clue what that meant. Anyway, let's get on with the story.

My first glimpse of Gawain came through the windows of an ancient wooden coach at the end of a mixed train towed by a puffing, belching black monster. Smoke clouded my view and ashes rattled against the soot-streaked pane as if trying to assault my nose as I pressed it against the inside of the glass. Memories from early childhood aren't the most reliable or complete, but some seem destined to cling with the permanence of a birthmark.

The Sandsend

Actually, my recall goes back even further to a rose garden behind a tiny cottage in Norfolk. While Junior and I played in the yard, our parents carefully packed boxes and suitcases in preparation for the move to Canada. Confused by the upheaval, I peeked in the back door and saw my blanket and rag doll disappear into a trunk. I began whimpering and tears ran down my cheeks and dropped off my chin.

Understanding my concern, Mother retrieved Rags from the trunk, squatted down before me, wiped away my tears, and put Rags in my arms. "Don't worry Stan," she said. "We'll have a bigger house in Canada with all our things in it. First we'll get on a big boat and travel for two weeks across the ocean. You'll have a nice bed in a cabin and eat in a dining room with the captain. And you can keep Rags with you all the time."

Although my mind couldn't comprehend or merge the disparate pictures of a boat, a cabin, and a dining room, I returned to the yard to play. But a knot slowly formed in my stomach—two weeks in a strange place without my blanket and toys sounded like eternity.

The next clear image out of my past reveals two little boys, their parents, and Aunt Dolly climbing into a rowboat to start the journey across the Atlantic. I'll tell you more about Aunt Dolly later. Two men in blue uniforms began pulling at heavy oars. Water sloshed back and forth about our feet with each roll of the boat.

Terror bubbled to the surface as I imagined two weeks in this tiny boat. I began to blubber, "Where's my *kip*, and the potty, and the *diming* room?"

The adults hushed me, not able to interpret my strange outpouring. But Junior, age four and smart in the ways of the world, knew how little kids thought—why just last year he'd been one himself. "Don't cry," he pleaded, "This baby boat is taking us to the big one out there. We're going to Canada on that great big boat."

The sailors pulled on the oars, moving us steadily forward. Pop said, "Stan, these men are sailors from the ship."

I stared at them in admiration, my fears forgotten. Waving Rags at one of them, I announced, "I gots a sailor suit too!"

"You'll have to wear it sometime," he answered.

Although he spoke to me, he gazed at Aunt Dolly, giving her a long up and down look—much like I'd seen Pop give to a new model racing bike. Then I noticed Pop's forehead wrinkle and his bushy eyebrows squeeze down close to his dark eyes as he glanced toward the sailor.

They rowed the boat right up to a steel wall rising straight out of the water. Mother, Junior, and Aunt Dolly scrambled up a rope ladder. I'm not sure how Pop did it, but suddenly I found myself flying up the ladder with Pop right behind me. As Aunt Dolly disappeared over the side, a seaman's strong arms reached down to pull me over. "Look out Aunt Dolly! Here I come," I yelled.

Then Pop vaulted over the rail, landing on the deck with a little bounce. We stood close together as a ship's officer approached and welcomed us.

Pop spoke, "I'm Fred Stone. This is my wife Harriet, my niece Dolly, and my sons Fred Junior and Stanley."

The officer grinned broadly as he shook Pop's hand. "Welcome aboard. But you're confusing me. You say these kids are your sons, and this lovely young lady is your niece, but I distinctly heard the little one call her Aunt Dolly."

Pop smiled back. "They are my sons and Dolly is my brother's daughter coming to Canada for a year-long visit. But due to the age difference and because they are proper British boys, Junior and Stan call her Aunt."

The officer shook Mother's hand and then turned to Aunt Dolly. He seemed to hold her hand for a long time before he turned to Junior and me, bowed slightly, and said, "We always enjoy having proper British gentlemen on board."

Pop's brow had furrowed up again. He said, "Thanks for letting us come aboard a day early. Had we waited until you docked tomorrow, it would have cost us extra for hotel rooms."

As we walked across the deck of the ship, I heard Mother say to Pop, "Quit worrying about Dolly. Sure, she's only five feet tall with a gorgeous peaches-and-cream complexion, but at 32 years old she's quite capable of taking care of herself."

I didn't understand that, so I wrinkled up my forehead just like Pop.

That evening, Mom suggested that Pop take me on a tour of the ship. I clung to Rags with one arm and put a viselike grip on Pop's index finger with my free hand. He pointed out the bridge where the ship's officers drove the ship, explained how the captain could talk to the engine room through voice tubes, showed me the dining room, even got permission to visit the engine room. "It's called a tramp freighter," he explained, "but it carries a few passengers. It costs a lot less than travelling on an ocean liner."

I didn't always understand everything Pop said, but I loved my Pop—I just knew he must be the smartest man in the world.

The next morning after our first breakfast with the ship's officers, we returned to the cabin. "Mommy, Mommy," I begged, "Hurry up or the boat will go without us."

"We're on the ship," she answered.

"He thinks being on deck is the boat, but not in here," Junior explained.

"In that case," Pop said, taking me by the hand. "Let's get on board the ship."

And so began a two-week, father-son adventure. The minute each meal ended, Pop took my hand and headed for the deck to take his constitutional with a tiny shadow at his side gripping a rag doll. We walked the decks in sun and rain, in smooth and rough weather. We watched for whales, talked to crewmen and explored every hidden recess of the vessel. Sometimes Junior came with us, but most of his time, he spent with Mother and Aunt Dolly.

One day while Pop held Rags for me and Mom and Aunt Dolly watched, two sailors swung Junior and me over the rail above a green sea. It scared me silly. I hung onto Pop's finger even more tightly after that.

We left the Sandsend the way we boarded her. A yellow motorboat carried us towards a dock tucked against the skyline of Montreal.

The journey west by train remains a blur until the conductor's cry of "Gawain" and the squeaking brakes prompted me to press my nose to the window.

I step into a new life

Junior and I stepped onto the station platform first. I cowered behind Junior's much bigger frame. Who were these strangers staring at us? I squeezed Rags tightly and felt tears building up, but before they started, Mom and Pop followed carrying the suitcases.

"Velcome back to Gawain," a grandfatherly man on the platform said to Pop. "I brought the team and vagon so ve can take you and your goods to the farm. It's great to have you back."

"Boys and Dolly," Pop said, "this is my good friend Johnny Johanson."

Grandpa shook our hands and welcomed us with his thick Norwegian accent, "Boys, your Pop calls me Yanny Yohanson, but you must call me Grandpa."

He turned back to Pop to ask, "Vill you start farming again?"

Pop stared across the village and prairie towards the distant, unseen homestead, then spoke, "Yes, I'll start again. It won't be easy; I'm over 60. But I've a young wife and family, a farm, and $6.00 in my pocket. We lost almost everything else we owned in England. Maybe I should never have left Canada four years ago to retire in England, but who could have predicted this awful depression?"

As we climbed into the wagon box with Grandpa Johanson, I heard a girl's voice say, "Those are the cutest little boys I have ever seen. I just love their English accents; And just look at the little doll in the sailor suit."

Grandpa turned to Junior and me and said, "Boys, this is my daughter Susan."

Susan, a dark-haired teenager, sat on a sack of grain and chatted with us as we rode through the countryside. At two and a half I couldn't fully appreciate her poise and beauty, but I decided I could like anyone who called me cute—even if she had called me a doll! Maybe life in Canada would be good after all. Especially when we could open the trunks and get out my blanket and toys so they could join Rags and me.

The Farm

After a few miles and two or three turns on straight, dirt roads, we descended into a coulee, entered a farm gate, then climbed through a gully, arriving back on the coulee bank at a farmstead overlooking three large ponds that reflected the azure sky. Grandpa Johanson stopped the wagon beside a two-story, frame house. A barn, chicken house, and long shed with sliding doors bordered the rest of the farmyard. When I looked for neighbouring houses but could see none, fear gripped me. I took a tight hold on mother's skirt and burst into tears.

Mother broke my grip, took my hand and said, "Come and see the house. Your father built it a long time ago."

We not only explored the house, but carried our belongings to the top floor where we would live until Sister June, her husband and two kids moved out. Even though she was the same age as Mother,

June really was my sister—a half-sister—a child of Pop's first marriage. But I didn't understand all that.

I also met my half brother Willie and his wife Jessie when they came over to welcome us. They lived on a farm adjoining ours. Willie had red hair. He looked a lot like Pop and moved very quickly, like a little bird. Jessie, who had blond hair, seemed taller and heavier than Willie. Even then, I thought, "She's the boss!"

They had their three kids with them, Reggie—about Junior's age—and Sadie and Orton—a lot older. Orton put on a silly grin, stared down at me, and said, "Hello Uncle Stan."

Uncle? I screwed up my face and backed away. I heard them talking about another half brother and a half sister who lived somewhere far away—talk about a confusing family!

The house fascinated me more than all these new family members. I remember best the windows. Each room on the ground floor had at least one set of huge double windows. Rooms on the second floor had one or two large single windows. In comparison, our house back in Norfolk had peep holes.

I hear the voices of little men

We hadn't been more than two or three days in the two-story house on the coulee bank when I made a discovery that would later change my life. Even at this point it gripped my imagination. In a smaller downstairs room, Sister June and Uncle Nate, Sister June's husband, kept a wooden box on a small table.

By the way, back then kids spoke formally to most adults calling them Mr., Miss, or Mrs. Those we knew well we called Aunt or Uncle if no other title seemed appropriate, except for Brother Willie and Aunt Jessie. For reasons I never figured out, we always called them just plain Willie and Jessie.

Anyway, Sister June and Uncle Nate's box had a row of knobs across the front and a variety of wires running from it. One day I crept into the room dragging my blanket with one hand while the other grasped Rags. Pop and Uncle Nate had pulled chairs up to the box. Both wore odd little black cups over their ears with wires connecting the cups to the wooden box. When Uncle Nate saw me, he removed the cups from his ears and placed them on mine. I heard tiny voices and immediately guessed they came from wee men hiding in the box. But when I asked Pop to lift the lid so I could see them, he and Uncle exploded in laughter. Well one day I would look in that box and figure out how it worked.

The two men listened for a few moments longer, then Pop spoke to Uncle Nate: "Do you think Bible Bill Aberhart will ever pay his $25 basic dividend to each Alberta resident? We could sure use that money."

Uncle Nate shook his head sharply, clapped his hands over the black things on his ears, and leaned closer to the box.

A moment later he sat up straight and turned to Pop who said. "So you think not?"

"I was shaking my head to hush you up Pop (like I said, everybody called my father Pop). I just wanted to hear the rest of the news. I don't know if he can do it, but I'll tell you one thing, Premier Aberhart and the Social Credit Party have got Ottawa and those eastern bankers scared. Things have changed in Alberta during your time away."

I slipped quietly from the room, dangling Rags by one leg and dragging my blanket through the dust and dead flies that often littered the floors of prairie farmhouses as the spring sun warmed the building.

Just weeks short of my third birthday, in awe and embarrassment, I had discovered the world of telecommunications—a world that would shape the 20th century and consequently become a central theme in my life. But more important, radio brought a new dimension to living in isolated communities. The listeners could now attend concerts, political functions, and get up-to-date news from the next town or from faraway lands. Radio had begun to break the terrible isolation of the prairies. Less than a quarter century earlier Pop had travelled 40 miles to the nearest town to get groceries and buy a newspaper. Now the little men in the box brought the world to the living rooms of remote farmsteads.

The house that Pop built

Pop had arrived in Alberta from England in 1907 to claim 160 acres located 40 miles or two days by horses and wagon from the nearest railway. He knew they planned to build a railway nearby and hoped the few shacks clustered around the Gawain post office would become a real town. Pop knew little about farming, but two years in the Anglo-Boer War had infused him with a spirit of adventure. While working for an established farmer in order to learn the ropes, he began to gather horses, plows, and the other tools of farming. Within two years he built a sod house beside a large slough on his own land and moved in with his wife and four kids.

The sod house, or *soddy*, squatted close to the ground. Its thick turf walls kept out the worst of the cruel Alberta winters. Pop lined the floor, walls, and ceiling with lumber he purchased and hauled from a town on the distant railway line. He fitted a window and door and installed a huge cast-iron cooking range. The range cooked the food, heated the water and warmed the single large room. They stored their belongings in trunks and crates. A table and chairs and home-made bunks completed the furnishings. They settled in for two uncomfortable, crowded, stuffy years.

Two years later Pop built the house with the help of a Swedish carpenter named Swenson. Pop sketched out a plan on a clean new board. Swenson looked it over, nodded his head and said, "Ya, by yimminy, ve can do it."

"Big windows. We want big windows," Pop instructed Swenson. The two worked at fever pace, for Pop didn't plan to spend another winter in a tiny, dismal sod shack. With the help of a team of horses pulling an earth scoop and friendly neighbours with picks and spades, they dug a cellar for the coal furnace. Swenson and Pop hand-mixed field stone and cement for a foundation and laid the beams to support the house. They soon completed the outer walls and raised and shingled the roof. Neither Pop nor Swenson knew anything about modern insulation.

Early one morning Pop arrived to find Swenson circling around the unfinished house shaking his head and muttering in Swedish. Each time he passed a pile of planks he struck it with his hammer and muttered "God bless us!" The pious Seventh day Adventist would say nothing stronger.

Pop watched the strange behaviour for a few moments, then spoke, "What's wrong?"

Swenson struck the lumber pile once again before saying, "By yimminy, ve forgot to put in the stairs!"

Pop roared with laughter. Neither of them had even thought of stairs! Together they decided to put them in the kitchen against the outside wall. The stairs turned sharply right at the top to enter a big room on the second floor previously planned as a master bedroom. That room became a common room with doors opening to three bedrooms. He called the common room "the landing."

It took hours to remove the double windows from each floor now traversed by the new flight of steps. The kitchen, located below the landing, had become long and narrow with only half the windows originally planned.

Down those stairs

Oh how I remember one of my earliest experiences with those stairs! Soon after we moved in, before Sister June and her family had moved from the lower floor, I decided to visit them. The top three steps made a right-angle turn, meaning the side of each step against the wall became very wide, while the side of the step against the banister narrowed to a point. Gripping Rags in my right hand, I tried to wrap my pudgy fingers around the bannister support pole. I say tried, because they spanned less than half the pole's circumference. I looked down, way down to the piles of dirty laundry on the lower steps and the open door at the bottom. Mother had begun preparing to do the weekly wash.

I bravely stepped from the landing to the top step, but my foot skidded off the narrowed step and my fingers released their tenuous grip. I wrapped both arms around Rags and rolled downward—my height just nicely matching the width of the stairs. Each time my body rotated I saw Mother on the top step, arms and legs akimbo, and mouth wide open. She held that stance as long as I could see her—until the laundry wrapped itself about my body. As I hit the bottom step, Sister June scooped me up and began unwinding the underwear, shirts, socks and pillowcases.

My spectacular descent didn't cause a single pain or bruise. Out of character, I didn't cry, not even a whimper. Indeed, I began to laugh! Could it be that I had begun to grow up?

Windows on a new life

Awakened by thunder, I crawled from bed and padded to the window where I stood transfixed at a world exploding with fire. Great sheets of yellow and blue light danced back and forth across the horizon while clouds hurtled bolts of fire at each other and at the helpless earth below. Great jagged branches of lightning, beginning high in the heavens hidden beyond the top of the window, bent and twisted their way earthward until they exploded into the prairie. The panes of glass shook with the noise of all-out battle. I stood in awe for a minute, then blurted, "God is fighting the debbil!"

"No, it's just an old thunder and lightning storm," said Junior who had quietly moved up beside me. "Pop told me Alberta has real bad lightning storms."

Junior had become a know-it-all the moment he learned to talk.

I hadn't completely recovered from that night of heavenly fire when the big windows brought me a day of darkness and fear.

Noel, a recent British immigrant who worked as a farmhand for a neighbour, had come to "see" Aunt Dolly. They sat chatting in the dining room. Not that Noel did much talking; he seemed to enjoy just sitting and listening. I liked Noel even though he got the same look on his face when he talked to Aunt Dolly as the sailors on the ship.

Aunt Dolly chased me from the dining room, so I drove my green toy car across the kitchen, following the roads drawn out by the pattern in the linoleum.

Just as I turned at the cook stove and gave a realistic "vroom, vroom," someone yelled, "There's one coming! Close things up."

Pop and Noel hurried outside to close the shed and barn doors while Mom and Dolly raced about the house closing windows and lighting oil lamps. Within minutes the storm smothered the sun in swirling blackness and began clawing at the house. The adults gathered in the dining room, waiting like soldiers prepared for action but not knowing what duty might demand or where the enemy might strike. I sat motionless on the kitchen floor gripping my precious toy.

"That window is going to go!" Pop yelled. Pop and Noel stared helplessly at the glass panes gyrating within their frames. Mother raced from the room, returning quickly with an armful of pillows.

"Hold these against the glass," Mom ordered. The men shook off their inaction and pushed the pillows to the trembling glass. Noel, being much taller than Pop, held two against the upper panes of the window. Lamp in hand, Aunt Dolly began an inspection of the rest of the house to make sure the storm hadn't forced its way through another window.

Dirt began seeping under the back door, creeping toward me. When Mother saw it, she grabbed a kitchen towel, dunked it in the crock that held drinking water and laid it across the bottom of the door. I remained on the floor, shaking all over.

Eventually the storm subsided. Pop and Noel went out to assess the damage while the women began to clean up dirt that had crept through a thousand tiny fissures around windows. I hadn't even cried! I returned my car to the lino highway, made a neat turn around the stove leg and began to "vroom, vroom" my way back across the kitchen.

The coulee

Stairs and windows aside, no part of early life on the farm fills as many spaces in my album of memories as our coulee.

Coulees, or small valleys, usually with fairly steep sides, wend across prairie lands. Some contain rivers or streams, but many see water only during spring runoff. Our coulee measured over 600 yards from the crest of one bank to the other. It arced through the northeast corner of the quarter section of land that Pop had claimed as a homestead and continued for miles in each direction, winding across other farms. But nowhere did it have the width and beauty of our coulee.

The ponds made it special—large ponds that remained full in all seasons. The largest almost touched the banks on either side. Two smaller ponds and acres of bulrushes filled the rest. Between the ponds gooey sinkholes, surrounded with rushes and sometimes covered with water, waited to pull the rubber boots off a straying child, or suck a careless cow or horse to its belly or beyond in black, smelly mire.

Despite the minor dangers of the sink holes, I'm sure Pop selected the site because he saw the potential of year-round water and a place that would support a small herd of cattle.

Although I didn't realize it during that first summer, the coulee and ponds would become my playground. Narrow cattle paths snaked through the waist-high, reddish-brown buck brush and silver sage that thickly covered the banks. They arrived eventually at the muddy edge of the biggest pond. We would race barefooted along the trails unconcerned about occasional encounters with skunks and porcupines.

In the spring we'd search out bird's nests—redwing blackbirds in the acres of bulrushes, crows and magpies in the willows and poplars, and water birds near the water. Catching tadpoles in tin cans and studying them and noting their various stages of development complemented our education. We always threw them back; we loved the sound of thousands of frog voices blending with the calls of birds and the rush of wind through bulrushes and willows.

Summertime brought out the dragonflies; these helicopters of the insect world fascinated us. We'd walk knee deep in water and mire amid the reeds to reach their habitat. Seated on the edge of the wooden culvert that allowed water from the smallest pond to escape down coulee, we'd watch muskrats at work and play near their beaver-like lodges. We imagined swimming with them, entering the underwater tunnel into their homes, and enjoying a friendly visit.

In the fall we'd study birds returning south. We looked especially for cranes, hoping to see the survivors of the ill-fated and dwindling flock of whooping cranes. Thousands of ducks of a dozen varieties converged on the ponds. We'd slip up to the water's edge and toss a stone to experience the thundering takeoff of countless birds.

They'd speed along just above the water, webbed feet running on the surface to give added thrust until they gained flying speed.

Winter found Fred Junior trapping weasels and rabbits in the animal runs that crisscrossed the coulee bottom and banks. Together, we'd follow the footprints of rabbits and coyotes across snow-covered, frozen ponds, up the banks, and across the fields. We soon learned to identify the tracks of other creatures who dared intrude into our world.

Most certainly, it became our world. We rarely shared it with others, except when friends and neighbours joined us to toboggan down the slopes and skate on the ponds.

Starting over

During the first year back on the farm, Mom and Pop did everything possible to get income rolling in. Pop bought a team of horses and put a few pigs and two cows in the barn. We always had plenty of milk to drink. Mom separated the cream and made butter, feeding the leftover skimmed milk to the hogs. Pop butchered them and Mom cured the bacon and ham in large earthenware crocks filled with brine. Mom also planted a big garden and filled the cellar with a year's supply of carrots, beets, potatoes, and squash. We did not lack food.

To earn cash before he could bring the farm into full production, Pop drove a horse-drawn school van. I often rode along with him, strengthening the special bond that had begun on the ship. I rode proudly between Pop and noisy boisterous school kids and got a view of the school life that lay ahead. One day a powerful wind blew the wooden van from its rubber-tired running gear and sent it rolling across a field. Pop got some cuts and bruises but no serious injuries. Fortunately, I hadn't gone with him that day.

Pop had some other near disasters. One of our cows, old Bessie, absently chewing her cud, decided to take a shortcut back to the barn by travelling through the coulee bottom and angling across the corner of the middle pond. Two cow-lengths into the water, the gooey, black, prairie muck ceased to support her weight. Her four pointy feet sank in beyond her knees—she fought back, driving herself deeper. When she finally gave up the battle only her head, neck and the top of her shoulders protruded above water. She decided to wait for rescue but, being a cow, she could at least redeem the time by chewing her cud.

Eventually, Pop found her and summoned neighbours to assist. We had only two cows; losing Bessie would create hardship. Grandpa Johanson and his hired man arrived wearing rubber boots, driving a team of draught horses, and carrying yards of heavy rope. An hour later, after many outbursts in English and Norwegian, much pulling by the horses, pushing by the men, and mooing by Bessie, the stranded cow burst free with a loud sucking sound. Lucky cow: she suffered little more than a sore neck and rope burns.

Just about that time we visited a neighbour whose farm dog had a litter of puppies.

"You can have one Stan. Just pick one out."

I stared at Mom in disbelief.

"Go ahead," she said.

I picked the little one—"the runt" someone called it. That's how Tippy joined our family. When he grew, he developed the tail and coat of a collie and the floppy ears of a spaniel. His legs didn't develop much at all—they remained short and crooked. He looked . . . silly, but we loved each other.

Pop makes a bed

Fred Junior, born before our parents four-year sojourn in England, often speculated on my origin, suggesting my real parents still lived in England, or that Mom and Pop had found me under a gooseberry bush. Maybe it had something to do with what Mom had said—about Fred having his nose out of joint. Anyway, it worried me until Pop did something that convinced me I really belonged. He made my bed!

No, Pop didn't just straighten the pillow and tuck in the sheets. He made the whole thing from scratch. With money desperately scarce, Mom couldn't order everything we needed from the Eaton's catalogue. I needed a bed, so Pop built it. Rummaging around through junk and leftovers on the farm, Pop found the head and foot boards of an old wooden crib. Two used two-by-twos became bed rails when screwed between the end pieces. He didn't paint them; I doubt he had either sandpaper or stain. A search of the drive shed provided material for the "springs"—enough chicken wire to stretch twice between the rails.

Grandma Johanson provided the next key element—an empty tick for a mattress. Pop carefully stuffed it with fresh straw and, behold, a bunk suitable for a prince. Pop's creation lasted only a few years—until my increasing weight began breaking through the chicken wire. By then my parents had a few more dollars and bought a real bed. But, I didn't forget what Pop had done for me. He loved me!

Precious water

As a lad under three, moving from civilized and cultured England to a prairie farm in the midst of the great depression, I received many shocks and had much to learn. True, the new house had lots of windows, an upstairs, eight rooms, and a radio. But in that era our house, like many others, had no running water, no plumbing, no electricity, and no adequate insulation or heating system.

Lack of running water meant that Pop daily carried two large pails from the well at the bottom of the gully. He'd pour those into a huge earthenware crock in the kitchen. An enamelled metal dipper floated on the water in the crock, its handle protruding over the rim. Anytime we felt thirsty, we'd simply drink directly from the dipper.

On wash or bath days, Pop carried extra water to fill the stove's reservoir and two or three large metal pots that Mom used to heat water on the stove top. Mom did the laundry right in the kitchen. With sleeves rolled up, she'd bend over a scrubbing board propped into one end of a square washtub filled with soapy water. Sometimes Pop would help her wring the clothes by hand and dump them into another washtub for a rinse and another hand wringing. Mother usually accompanied her washday by singing. Her mezzo-soprano voice filled the house with song—either a hymn or an old army ditty, depending on her mood.

Lack of plumbing meant that Mom scrubbed us in a washtub on Saturday night. No, she did not use the scrub board! As she did for washday, Mom set up near the kitchen stove so she could easily ladle hot water from the stove's reservoir into the tub. While she got things ready, Fred and I would strip off our clothes and streak back and forth through the yellow light from the oil lamps. We'd run the length of the big room, enjoying the rush of air over our naked bodies.

Having no electricity meant we used kerosene to fuel glass-chimney lamps for the house and hurricane lanterns for the barn. On special occasions we would light up an Aladdin mantle lamp. As winter drew on, I learned about unheated bedrooms. But while I could handle most inconveniences, the lack of plumbing, of a proper toilet, got to me.

The outhouse

I can't recall my first trip to the privy or outhouse, although it surely happened before my third birthday. I certainly remember later visits: the two gaping maws ready to conduct the careless into the bowels of the earth, my nose twitching and rebelling until I gagged from the stench, and the sound of rusty hinges and the brush of cobwebs on my forehead. By age four, I had graduated from the chamber pot and began making daily pilgrimages down the path to the little outhouse at the edge of the grove.

The tiny wooden building, small enough that a half-grown child could almost touch all four sides without moving, contained a wall-to-wall wooden bench or seat. The seat had two side-by-side holes cut into it, a bigger one for adults and a smaller one for kids. A pile of newspapers and an old Eaton's catalogue occupied a corner, not for reading, but for what we called "ammunition."

Some outhouses had wooden lids covering the holes, but not ours. And here the terror began. As I sat on the small hole, straining hard to quickly finish my business and escape the stench, my imagination would run wild. What if I fell through the hole and sank helplessly into the slime and ooze beneath? I'd heard of kids stumbling out to the privy at night, sitting on the big hole by mistake, slipping in, and disappearing forever.

During evenings, I'd carry a lantern to keep coyotes at bay as I raced for the outhouse. Once inside in the oily yellow light of the lantern, I would imagine something worse than a coyote, a prehistoric slime monster down below, reaching up to grab me. Even worse, in the midst of winter I expected hoar frost or icicles to form on my unprotected bottom.

During one winter, I had a stroke of genius. I would quit going to the outhouse, at least for number two. Days, maybe weeks, slipped by before I confided in my big brother. Being a year and a half older, Fred Junior had a better knowledge of physical processes, so he blabbed to mother.

Mother had studied practical nursing and knew what to do. She had all the needed equipment on hand and quickly got to the bottom of the problem. It took a full week and numerous enemas and soapy suppositories to flush clean all the blocked passages. (It took decades to outgrow the damage I'd done.) I'd learned two lessons: don't try to ignore nature, and don't trust Fred Junior with a confidence.

A big mouth at the wedding feast

Noel showed up often during our first year on the farm. He seemed to appear in time to help Pop finish the chores. Then he'd come in for a cup of tea and a scone that Mother had pulled out of the oven earlier in the day. Even I had figured it out. Noel didn't come for the fellowship or the food—he came to see Aunt Dolly.

They held the wedding in our house. I can't remember a thing about the ceremony, but I sure do remember the wedding dinner—they likely called it a wedding supper back then. The adults added leaves to our dining-room table, then stuck the kitchen table at the end to seat about 16 people in all. Mother covered the whole thing with white cloths and set out her best dishes—augmented by extra settings borrowed from a neighbour.

The table and setting have nothing to do with the incident forever lodged in my memory. I remember it because it turned everyone's ears and eyes in my direction. I sat near the corner on the long side of the table right next to the Reverend Mr. Wiebe.

The bride and groom sat on the far side near the middle with two other people flanking them. Seated on a regular chair, my mouth barely made it to the edge of the table, so I could just see the bride and groom over my plate. Two or three other people, including the teen-age Susan Johanson, bustled about with serving trays and platters of meat, potatoes, and squash. Susan had remained special to me, beginning the moment I met her on the railway platform as we stepped off the train.

"Shall we ask the blessing?" said the pastor. Peering across my still-empty plate, I watched the heads bow and eyes close, all except those belonging to Noel.

"Our heavenly Father . . .," began the prayer. In fascination I watched Noel eyeing his bride. Would he ever tire of looking at her?

"Bless this food to our bodies . . .," the prayer continued. Noel now shifted his eyes to the pastor, then let them slowly circle the table, studying each guest in turn.

The prayer finished, "In the name of our Lord, Amen." All heads lifted and eyes opened, but a silence rested on the room for one or two seconds before a tiny voice intruded.

"Noel had his eyes open," I called out from my lowly position.

Aunt Dolly immediately accused, "How could you tell unless you had yours open too."

The truth of her statement dawned on me and I dropped down behind the edge of the table as if to duck the laughter that bounced off the four walls and ceiling.

Lost on the prairie

Not long after Aunt Dolly married Noel, Susan Johanson married Eric Pederson. The newlyweds moved onto a farm on the next road over so that it abutted at the rear of Grandma and Grandpa Johanson's place. Being technically clever, Eric built a telephone system between the farms. He powered discarded radio horns with telephone batteries and stretched wire along a mile and a half of fence line.

On visits to the Johanson's, Grandma would let us rap inside the horn with a spoon. That would bring Susan to the horn at her end so we could carry on a conversation.

We didn't get out much, so when Grandma and Grandpa Johanson asked us to join them for supper and a visit to Susan and Eric's place, we happily went along.

After eating, we all piled into Grandpa's tiny van to drive in the winter darkness the mile-and-a-half across the fields to the young couple's farm. The little van would run along easily on sleighs behind the team—even on the deep snow that had fallen in the last few days. Grandma Johanson in her thick accent asked Grandpa, "Think you can find de vay, Yonny, in the dark and snow?"

He just laughed, "Vat are you saying voman? Get lost in my own fields?"

Then he hooked two big alligator clips onto a car battery by his feet. An old car headlight fixed on the roof of the van shone a beam across the yard, "Get lost vit dat? No vay."

We drove past the barn and out the back gate with sleigh bells jingling and snow crunching under the runners. After a few minutes Grandma said, "Shouldn't ve have reached de east fence by now, Yonny?"

"No," Grandpa answered. But then he pulled up the team and stared out the tiny window in the front. The rest of us couldn't see much of anything. "Funny, someone's been trew here by sleigh recently. Who'd be driving around in our field? Must've been the Ellis boys getting a load of straw—I said they could take vat dey vanted."

Grandpa chucked-up the horses and we went on for a few more minutes before he stopped again and said, "Look at dat. More tracks going de other direction. These tracks look even fresher. The boy's must be lost out here. Maybe dey'll see our light and follow us."

In another five minutes Grandpa stopped again and said, "Ve just crossed more new tracks and now ve've come to a fence—but there shouldn't be a fence here!"

"Just sit tight Yonny," Grandma said and climbed out the door at the back.

She put her head back in after a moment and said, "Yonny,

ve're up against de nort fence. You've been driving in circles and crossing your own tracks. Follow me."

We peeked out the tiny window to see that old, wiry, tough, little Scandinavian grandmother walking in the beam of the headlight. She took us through deep snow banks, across the field, and straight to the exit gate and the lane on the far side. When she got back in she never reproved her husband, she just said, "Ve're okay now Yonny."

There's no party like a political party

At one time in at least one part of Canada, people turned politics into fun and games. The Social Credit meeting once highlighted the winters in rural Alberta for kids and adults. I really shouldn't speak for adults, but as a preschooler back then, nothing apart from Christmas excited me more.

The fun started when Mom and Pop hurried through evening chores, then prepared for the outing. Like most of our neighbours, we travelled during winter in a horse-drawn open box mounted on runners. While Pop threw some straw on the bottom, mother gathered quilts and blankets. Straw and bedding created a cosy nest for Junior and me. Mother put a kitchen chair near the front, positioning it where she could keep an eye on us and still watch Pop's driving. Seated on the chair and wrapped in a travel rug she could just peek over the front for a view of the road, hindered somewhat by the horses' rumps. Pop took the position favoured by most prairie men—standing upright. That way he got a good view but exposed the upper half of his body to the weather.

In the pitch black of a mid-winter evening, we snuggled into our nest, Mother checked the blankets, and Pop hollered gitty-up. Cold, black nights amplify sound, especially to the ears of a child viewing the world as a four-by-ten foot section of starry sky. The rhythmic sound of sleigh bells combined with the slapping and jingling of harness leather and metal fixtures. The crunch of horses' hoofs on crisp snow vied with the hiss of runners breaking a new track.

When a mysterious blue-white light caught our attention, Fred and I abandoned our covers and stood up to watch the northern lights dancing across the heavens. From this vantage point we also began a search for our other night-time favourites, the Big Dipper and Orion. Mother, herself enchanted by the stunning winter display, allowed us a few minutes before ordering us back under the covers with a warning; "You'll freeze your noses. It's twenty below out here."

At the Johanson farm, mother bundled us quickly into the house while Pop took the horses to the shelter of a barn or driving shed. The meeting wouldn't start until more people arrived, but those already there had begun socializing. Knowing I had little time, I too began the rounds.

In one corner I found a group of men throwing rubber sealer rings at a thing that looked like a dart board, but with cup hooks positioned to catch the rings. Soon bored with this, I moved on. In the living room a group of older children, girls, gathered around a piano while one showed off her skill by plinking out Twinkle, Twinkle Little Star. I finally found the boys in the mud room trying their skills on a couple of mouth organs. They soon chased me away but let my brother stay. I carefully avoided the women gathered in the kitchen—no need to remind Mother my bedtime passed two hours ago.

Back in the living room, I met Eric. The young farmer had many talents. Tonight he balanced a concertina on his knee and with some effort began coaxing music from the ancient instrument. I watched with fascination as his hands moved back and forth working the bellows while at the same time his fingers pushed an array of buttons.

When he finished his practice session and put the instrument aside for the sing-song to come later, I turned my attention to a group of men already deep in serious political discussion. One said, "Those Easterners have done it again. If they don't like the laws we pass, they simply declare them *ultra vires*."

"Whatever that means," said another. "They likely just made the word up to keep Alberta under control."

Responding to a sudden commotion at the door, a third man said, "The MLA just got here. Time to get the meeting under way."

Suddenly my whole body shot upwards, turned horizontally, and rocketed head first through the crowd. Mother had found me, grabbed me suddenly from behind, and popped me playfully under one arm. In minutes she took me upstairs, undressed me, put on my pyjamas, and placed me with other children lined up sideways across a big bed. Within seconds I fell sound asleep; for me the party had ended.

I awoke the next morning at home in my own bed.

Although my political training had begun, I still had to learn that the word *party* when used politically doesn't usually refer to fun and games.

Green feed

The following spring Mother went into the hospital in Gawain for reasons I can't remember—possibly a bout of pneumonia. She used to get pneumonia or bronchitis almost every year.

Pop didn't possess many domestic skills. He didn't want to cart Junior and me back and forth to the hospital when he visited Mom, so he asked the newlyweds, Aunt Dolly and Noel to help out. At that time they lived a mile over on the next road toward Gawain at Willie and Jessie's house during a time when Willie had taken a job training horses in Edmonton. Aunt Dolly came over every day to feed us and look after the house.

On her shopping day she left Fred Junior in Pop's care and took me home with her. At noon Noel came in from the fields. Following lunch and a half-hour nap, he hooked his best horse, Beauty, to a buggy and we set off for town. Beauty had needed the lunch-hour break as much as Noel; she had spent the morning with her teammate pulling a binder, cutting green oats for use as animal feed. Because Noel believed that the ox (or the horse) is worthy of its hire, he had let Beauty pig out on the fresh "green feed."

While Mom and Pop would have squeezed me between them on the seat, the honeymooners didn't want anyone coming between them. They placed me on a low stool between their feet and the dashboard, with my head just high enough to get a good view of Beauty's backside. We swung out of the yard and onto the dirt road on a glorious day with the smell of new-mown hay and green oats permeating the air.

I actually saw it coming, but couldn't move fast enough to get out of the way. Indeed, I had no place to go in any case. Beauty raised her tail and let loose a stream of green manure that poured over the dashboard and engulfed me from head to toes. While Dolly wiped my face with a handkerchief, Noel swung the buggy back homeward. Dolly didn't wait to heat water; she dunked me, protesting and screaming, into a washtub-full drawn straight from the well. Noel cleaned up the buggy, collected Dolly's shopping list, and headed for town.

Oh, but the embarrassment didn't stop there. Dolly heated water and washed the green manure from shirt, pants, socks, and underwear—yes, and even my shoes. I had no change of clothing, so she dressed me in her bathing suit. Thanks to Aunt Dolly's tiny stature, it almost fitted. In fear that someone might see me dressed, or half dressed, in a woman's clothing, I spent the rest of the day hiding under the dining room table, emerging every half hour to ask of my clothes flapping on the line, "Are they dry yet?"

Changes and coming change

I quickly recovered from the liquid manure and the embarrassment, but the excitement in Aunt Dolly and Noel's life reached a peak. That summer Willie and Jessie wanted their place back because Willie gave up his city job to return to farming. Noel took the change in stride. After a long discussion with Pop, he bought a farm about two miles north of our place. Then to cap off their summer the stork brought them a little baby. They called her Emily.

Both Fred Junior and I grew—Junior much more than I. He always outweighed me enough to demand my respect. Pop got much more involved in running the farm although he still leased out the land. The summer and harvest passed, and winter returned again. About a month before Christmas, Mom made an announcement. We would soon have a new baby in our house too!

"It will be like having a new doll in the house—a living doll," Mother said.

I'd long since relegated Rags to the back of the closet, so I wondered why Mom wanted a doll of her own. Anyway with Christmas so close who wanted to think about babies?

A startling revelation

Within months of our arrival on the farm, Sister June, Uncle Nate, and their two children had moved on to British Columbia. Since then Junior and I had the run of the whole house. During the winter months when the weather kept us indoors, we used the big upstairs landing as a playroom.

Since Sister June had taken their radio with the earphones, Pop had replaced it with one equipped with a loudspeaker so the whole family could hear. Mom would let us listen for an hour each day; buying batteries cost too much to run it more.

One Saturday, with snow crystals still beating against the window and the tension of approaching Christmas in the air, I sprawled on my stomach on the landing floor and began leafing through old magazines, "reading the pictures."

I turned a page of *The Saturday Evening Post* and saw Santa Claus scowling at me as though I'd landed on his bad-boy list. He stared angrily from a doorway occupying one third of the page—the right side of the right-hand page. Funny, how traumatic moments remain in the nooks of our minds the way old family pictures clutter odd corners of our homes.

Startled by Santa's out-of-character appearance and unable to read the text under the picture, I pointed to him and said aloud, "What's wrong with Santa?"

Junior-become-Fred placed his seven-year-old hand on Santa's face. "There's no such person as Santa," he proclaimed.

"Is too!" I yelled back.

"Is not!"

"Is too! I'll ask Mommy. She knows."

Mother conveniently climbed the stairs and entered the landing, possibly to determine the reason for the yelling. "Mommy," I demanded, "Fred Junior says there's no Santa. Tell him there is."

Mother didn't lie.

My childhood Christmas myth crashed down around me. I stumbled back to the window feeling vulnerable, wishing I could grow a thick icy crust to keep the world out, a crust as thick as that developing on the snow drifts under the hand of a freezing, dry wind.

Christmas

Mom and Pop had returned to the farm in difficult times. Common with most others during the great depression, they had little money for extras like Christmas toys. We always hoped for many things but had learned to expect little.

Now with Santa dead my hopes dipped so low they almost equalled my expectations. But I'd carefully watched the groceries Mom got in town and knew we'd get an apple, an orange, and maybe some hard candy.

Christmas always arrived when we needed it most—at the coldest, darkest, lowest, nastiest time of winter—at the very bottom of winter's icy pit. In November it would gradually build its strength for a December onslaught. In January Chinook winds would begin to punch holes through its frigid walls. Thank God, the joy and excitement of Christmas, no matter how meagre, got us through winter's worst.

On Christmas Eve, driven snow slashed horizontally past the kitchen window, each snowflake a miniature buzz saw, every burst of gale-force wind carrying enough snow to hide the farmyard behind a wall of white hell. Even as a preschooler, I knew the danger of such a storm. I knew the rampaging snow would sting and cut and freeze exposed flesh. I could visualize the fence-high drifts that would stop cars and trucks and upset sleighs.

"Santa," I whispered, feeling every nerve tense within me. "How will you get through?"

Then I remembered, and the energy bled from each nerve. Santa isn't coming, because Santa, because Santa . . . isn't!

On Christmas morning in a second-floor bedroom, Fred and I awakened. We popped our heads from under the covers of the big double bed, our eyes growing large as we focused on stockings swollen with toys and goodies. For a moment our heads protruding from the covers didn't move as breath froze in the ill-heated room. Then we grinned and bounced toward stockings hanging on the foot of the bed.

We both retreated back under the covers to examine the loot. Cries filtered through the layers of blankets and patchwork quilts: "A cap gun, I gotta gun!" "I got one too!" "An apple and an orange!" "Look, nuts!" "I got crayons!"

Moments later, I emerged from the bed, landed on my knees on the floor, and pulled a chamber pot from beneath the bed. Before the tinkling sound ended, Fred threw back the covers, and with Christmas stocking under arm and toy pistol in hand, said, "Let's go down and see what's under the tree!"

"Wait for me!" I yelled. Although the rule said, "Wash before coming down in the morning," neither of us took time to break the ice in the wash basin.

Parcels under the tree provided wind-up trains for each of us and things for Mom and Pop. Mom said, "We've had a wonderful Christmas because Aunt Elsie sent a big box with things for each of us. The toy guns and trains had belonged to her boys. Without her help it would have been a bleak Christmas."

And I thought, "Mom and Fred Junior don't know everything. Santa lives! She calls herself Aunt Elsie."

The stork lands again

When Pop told me that Mom had gone to the hospital to get the new baby, I didn't know what to expect; I hadn't paid much attention to Aunt Dolly's baby. I'd seen a few kittens arrive with their eyes shut and a couple of calves that immediately stared out at the world through great brown eyes. I'd even begun to develop a farm boy's theory on the origins of babies.

Gosh, it was nasty and cold when Pop came by Grandpa and Grandma Johanson's where he'd left me for a few days while Mother went to the hospital. Pop jammed me into my winter clothes, pushed me out the door, and aimed me toward the cutter. He'd made it from an old roadster car body, so it didn't give much protection from the weather. Pop never carried me like Mom did;

but he did wait patiently while I struggled through the snow and wind, dragged open the metal door, and tumbled in.

We negotiated the coulee hills, the horse working hard, breath coming like steam escaping from a locomotive, but with much of it freezing on her face like a Halloween disguise. Pop drove the mare right into the machine shed before unhitching. Puffing clouds of steam myself, but more like a teakettle than a locomotive, I struggled through the snow to the house. Looking back I saw Pop watching me. As I went into the house, he turned to lead the horse toward the barn.

Inside the house Fred Junior met me, just bubbling with excitement. "Junior," Mom called from the next room, "help Stan get off his things."

Fred Junior tugged and I pulled. "Aw Mom," Junior yelled, "Pop put Stan's snow pants on backwards!"

My outer clothing with its crust of snow soon dropped in a heap on the kitchen floor. I took off for the front room that Mom and Pop had recently turned from a dining room into a bedroom. Mom sat on her bed with the living doll in her arms. "Her name is Joy, because she'll give me a lot of joy in life," she said.

I looked into a little red face. I noticed her tiny perfect hands with wee fingernails. I saw two big brown eyes gazing back at me. I thought of the baby kittens and calves in the barn, and sputtered, "Oh Mom . . . she's got . . . eyes . . . they're open already!"

As I said, I thought I had figured out where babies came from—so much for a farm boy's special knowledge. I actually got concerned for the overworked stork when I heard he had visited Susan and Eric's place to deliver another baby girl.

Meanwhile, back on the farm

Pop decided not to resume all the farming tasks. By leasing out the land to neighbours, they would provide the finances and equipment to put the crops in. Pop would get the proceeds from one-third of the crops. In addition to that income, he decided to raise a few cattle, pasturing them in the coulee and wintering breeding stock in the barn. He also converted part of the barn into a pig sty. Mother did her part by putting in a huge garden and raising chickens.

During the months between that great Christmas and the following summer, it looked like Pop, with a lot of help from Mom, would succeed in his plan to start over again. If things went well, he could pull us back from the grip of poverty. But often the best laid plans of mortals, like the crops they plant on the prairies, never reach fruition.

Pop begins to lose touch

Sometimes the momentous events that move like tornados through our lives start with the simplicity of a gentle summer breeze. I hadn't in my childhood innocence seen the shadows of the approaching life-changing storm, but Mom had.

When Noel and Aunt Dolly dropped in on the way into Gawain, I should have noticed the strain on the adults' faces, but I didn't. Pop sat at the kitchen table drinking a cup of tea, while Mom huddled with Noel and Aunt Dolly in the archway to the adjoining room. "Let's take him right now," said Noel, glancing toward Pop.

Mom nodded, walked over to Pop, placed a hand on his shoulder, and said, "Fred, Noel can take us to see the doctor right now. Let's go."

Pop gave Mom a strange, blank look, and turned to his full, steaming teacup.

"Finish your tea," Mom said.

Pop tipped the hot tea into his saucer and blew on it to cool it. He sipped a few mouthfuls before slamming down the cup and saucer, spilling tea on table and floor. Then he stood up, collected his hat from a peg near the door, and without a word headed for Noel's rig parked in the yard.

Mother mopped up the tea, picked up Joy, and followed him without uttering a word to anyone. Aunt Dolly called to Fred Junior and me, "Come on. We're all going."

We all piled into Noel's green wagon box mounted on the running gear of an old Star motor car. Mom put Joy on a blanket beside Emily—too young to play they stared and cooed at each other. Noel clucked at the team of bays, and we started briskly along the lane that led down the gully to our farm gate in the coulee bottom.

We left the gate and turned south on the dirt road, the clip-clop of the horses' feet ringing out from the sun-hardened earth. The team mounted the coulee hill and broke into a gentle trot. Noel slapped the reins across their backs and we began to fly along at a great rate.

I stood against the side of the wagon box with the wind rushing through my hair and watched a hawk circling against the clear late-August sky. Even as I studied the beauty of his soaring flight, he clamped wings to body and fell like a stone. His course carried him behind a thicket; I imagined the scream of a stricken creature and almost immediately the hawk reappeared, powerful wings driving him upward, a dying gopher gripped in his talons.

Beyond the fence, a three-horse team pulled a grain binder around the perimeter of a golden field. The chatter of cutters, the swish of wooden sails knocking down stalks of wheat, and the thumps of neatly-tied bundles ejecting from the machine drew my mind from the previous ominous scene of death.

Pop stood at the front of the wagon beside Noel. Staring straight ahead over the pulsating backs of the horses, he said, "A tonic. That's all I need, just a tonic. That'll fix me up."

We turned west onto the main road, past willows, sloughs, and gentle rises, common to this part of Alberta characterized as "prairie parkland." Beyond the road to Willie's place, we passed a large slough. The slightest of breezes barely stirred the surface, allowing us to see the reflection of one wispy cloud. The voices of hundreds of frogs serenaded us, overcoming the noise of horses hoofs and rubber wheels on the smooth dirt track. A sour smell of stagnant water mixed with the tangy odour of new-mown hay wafting from an adjacent field.

As we moved beyond the slough, Noel stiffened. He steered the team so close to the edge of the road the right wheels ran in the ditch. From behind I heard the uneven beat of a V8 coming fast. Glancing over my shoulder I saw the nose of a '32 Ford. It raced past at forty miles an hour, a rooster tail of dust following it.

"Idiot," Noel muttered.

Apart from that one word from Noel and Pop's comment about a tonic, none of us spoke during the journey. The adults had their minds on something I couldn't understand. But I really didn't notice, I'd been too occupied with wonder, with the life, death, toil, sights, sounds, and smells of the world around me. How could I know our happy little world would soon come apart?

Chapter 2

Change

Our lives turn upside down

As I said, Mother had seen it coming. A few months after Joy's birth, she realized Pop had begun to lose touch. He'd stare into a corner and talk about things long gone. He'd have fits of temper, then, just as quickly, return to normal. Mom watched as the condition slowly worsened. Pop's trips into the past got longer and the temper outbursts turned to rage. Mother, without communicating it to Fred Junior and me, began to live in terror. Or, perhaps Fred Junior, being a little older, did know, while I, always the dreamer, lived in my own world.

Anyway that trip to Dr. Rich settled the issue. He signed Pop into the mental hospital in Ponoka, Alberta. They said he had hardening of the arteries of the brain.

They didn't keep Pop in the hospital for long the first time. They sent him home and told Mother to make sure he didn't worry. He soon became ill again, but Mother kept him around until he became unmanageable. Then she had no option but to send him away again. That scenario repeated again and again. I don't remember how many times it happened before they kept him for good.

Almost no one in the community seemed able to help Mother. Noel wanted to but he would turn to jelly in Pop's presence when the illness struck. Other than the Johansons, most neighbours simply stayed out of our way. Then someone thought of Al Nixon.

Everyone said Al drank too much—they called him the town drunk. I couldn't figure that out, because I knew he lived on a farm just north of Gawain. Anyway, it seems he had a special way with people. Mom always said that Al understood other people's problems because of his own affliction. No matter how ill Pop became, Al could handle him like a baby. Mother would send out a call for Al, who would come and stay for a few days to look after

Pop until he and Mom realized Pop would get no better. Then they'd send for the police who would come for Pop and take him back to Ponoka.

Although much of that time remains a blur, I clearly recall a few incidents. I remember when Al Nixon hurried across the upstairs landing carrying a sheaf of papers. Then he sped down the stairs in answer to sharp military commands emitting from Pop's room. In less than three minutes he returned, labouring up the stairs, cheeks puffed and red, breath coming in great bursts. Al's excess weight and great beer belly certainly hindered when it came to hurrying up and down stairs.

He raced back into Pop's room. Again I heard Pop snapping out orders. And again Al hurried from the room, down the stairs and outside, only to return quickly. That activity continued all afternoon, ending only when Pop tired and went to sleep.

"What on earth are you doing?" Mom asked the wheezing, red-faced Al.

"He's back in the Boer War sending army dispatches. All I can do is humour him, so I deliver his dispatches to the General. You can't resist him when he's off like that; he has the strength of two men."

I remember another time when we heard Pop calling from his room. I followed Mom and peeked in. Had she seen me, she'd have sent me running with a cuffed ear. I saw Pop staring at the ceiling, cringing with the bed clothes pulled tightly under his chin. "Get them away! Get them away from me! Get those animals out of here."

The shingles had leaked. The rainwater stains on the ceiling created marvellous patterns—pictures that I could clearly see as lions and elephants and monkeys—I guess Pop could see them too. Somehow, Mom got Pop settled down. Once out of the room she wrote a note and handed it to Fred Junior. Take this to Willie's. Ask him to get it to Al Nixon as soon as possible. If he can't do that, maybe he can come himself because I need help. Mother knew some basic psychology; she knew Willie would saddle a horse and immediately ride for Al.

I remember a time when Pop stood at a mirror hung on the centre divide of the double windows in the kitchen. He had just finished trimming his mustache with a large pair of Mom's sewing scissors. Fred entered the room following a trip to town with Noel where he had done a few family errands. "Did you mail the letter to Aberhart?" Pop asked, turning partially toward Fred.

Mother hadn't given the letter to Fred. She didn't think Pop's appeal to the Alberta Premier appropriate.

"No," said Fred, completely unaware of the letter and Mother's subterfuge.

Pop spun completely around. Catching Fred by the shoulder, he raised the scissors like a dagger ready to strike. Mother moved quickly, grabbing Pop's wrist to stop the blow. "No." she yelled, "he's just a boy. It's not his fault."

That scene, outlined against the window, etched itself deeply into my mind. Fred leaped aside while Mom and Pop rocked to and fro until Pop finally gave up the scissors.

"Wow," I thought, "the strength of two men, but Mom won!"

Again and again, I witnessed similar altercations between Mom and Pop. Each time Mother realized she had waited too long before sending for Al or the police.

I remember, much too clearly, another struggle. I opened the door at the bottom of the stairwell to the landing, intent on finding Mom for a reason long forgotten. I looked up to see her, with her back to me, a step or two down the stairs. She stood facing Pop who seemed intent on pushing her aside or throwing her down the stairs. With her right hand gripping a newel post, Mother pushed and fought back with her left. Both stood just over five feet tall, but Pop, with the advantage of the steps, towered over her.

I should have moved out of the way before a body landed on me, but I stood mesmerized by the battle raging above. Slowly—arguing, pushing, pleading—Mom drove Pop back out of my sight onto the landing and into his room. That time I carried the "send Al Nixon" note across the fields.

We had no better way to get messages out. During the early years of Pop's illness, the farm ceased to function as a working farm. Mother had to sell Pop's team because she couldn't handle them, so we had no transportation. During the school year Mom could send a note to town by the school van. The driver or one of the school children would see it got to the appropriate people. Most often, and especially in an emergency, she would give it to Fred or me and send us scurrying to a neighbour's, the one she judged most able to help in the circumstances.

But Mom did have one secret weapon that helped her survive the nights.

When Pop came home from the hospital, Mom would light an oil lamp and keep it burning in an upstairs window. A mile away across the coulee Grandma Johanson would keep watch. As long as she could see the lamp, she knew mother needed no help. She would check it during the evening, at bedtime, first thing in the morning, and anytime she got up during the night. If she failed to see the lamp, she would assume we had a problem and rouse Grandpa Johanson who would pile into his '27 Chevrolet in the summer, or a cutter in the winter, and hurry over to offer assistance.

Invariably, after Grandpa or Al's intervention, Mother would concede defeat. Within a day or two, Fred Junior and I would stand at the garden gate and watch two police officers assisting Pop into the back seat of a car. The officers would cast troubled looks my way as I blubbered, "Please don't take my daddy away. Please don't take Pop."

Enter the opposition

During his first visit home from Ponoka, Pop wrote a will favouring Mother. He also gave her power-of-attorney so she could manage the farm. When one of Pop's children by his first wife heard about the new arrangements, he saw all future benefits of Pop's estate slipping from his grasp. Why should this usurper, the young bride, gain control? By lobbying the appropriate authorities, he succeeded in having them set aside both the will and the power-of-attorney based on Pop's supposed mental incompetence at the time of signing.

Accepting this view meant placing Pop's estate in the hands of the public administrator. He ruled that Mom could remain in the house, but made no provision for her support or that of the family.

Our financial status, always tenuous, now got much worse. But Mother's resourcefulness kept us going—her big garden, her baking and cooking skills, and her flock of poultry kept us from hunger. Fortunately, we had good neighbours who would help when they could, even though they had limited incomes and busy lives.

My turn to visit the doctor

During summers Fred Junior and I could always find lots to do. Come rain or shine we'd play in the machine shed, pushing open one of the six huge sliding doors wide enough to let in light. We'd crawl into the old threshing machine, mark out village streets in the loose dust that covered the shed floor, or build things from old machine parts and boards. The shed had hidden dangers, some as innocuous as dry splintered boards. One hot summer day, I stepped on one and drove a splinter deep into my bare foot. When I wouldn't let Mother touch it, she said, "Okay, off to the doctor we go."

Within the hour, Mother dragged me kicking and screaming through the doorway of a house in Gawain. We entered a small room furnished with rattan chairs. The room had three doors: the one we had entered from outside; a second standing partly open showed an adjacent living room; the third, a panelled wooden door, led to the horror chamber. I sat cowering against Mother, sobbing uncontrollably, but with one eye fixed on that third door.

Dr. Rich, a gentle-looking grandfatherly man, opened the door and waved us in. Mother entered briskly, carrying me head-first under one arm. She plopped me on a chair beside a desk; my sobbing intensified.

"What's wrong with him?" demanded the doctor as he seated himself behind the desk.

"He has a splinter in his foot and he won't let me get it out."

"Let's see it," said the oldster, taking my foot and unwinding the temporary bandage.

My first visit to a doctor's office had started badly; now it got worse. While the doctor poked about in a hole in the sole of my foot, I screamed and fought. He finally released my foot and barked at me, “Will you shut up!” and to Mother, “We’ll have to do this a little differently.”

He turned to a cabinet and picked up a huge syringe. To me it looked like a small drinking glass with a needle the size of a pencil protruding from one end. Again he and Mother combined forces to secure my foot. Sheer terror gripped me so that I stiffened like a board and couldn’t utter a word as he sunk the needle into my foot. I thought it penetrated all the way to my knee.

A few minutes later when the doctor began probing for the splinter, I could feel no physical pain. But the terror continued as he dug chunks of flesh away to reveal the splinter. I kept my eyes tight shut and continued to blubber. Mercifully, he soon finished and placed the splinter on the desk. I can see it today; to my distorted perception, it looked like a piece of chopped firewood.

As we left the office, Mother pushed her head into the living quarters to greet the doctor’s wife. She handed in a freshly-killed chicken wrapped in brown butcher’s paper—this in lieu of the doctor’s fee.

Mother, doctor, and I survived that experience. Over the next few years before we moved away and minor childhood problems required me to revisit that office, he would say, “I promise not to hurt you if you promise not to cry.”

Most of the time I didn’t.

Joy has her turn

Junior had started to school in September two or three months after Pop took ill. As a student in first grade, my big brother became very worldly-wise, even insisting we call him Fred, not Junior. But for me, things got mighty boring with Pop away and Fred in school—I had to learn to entertain myself. Even though it was a Saturday and Fred was home, I was doing just that when Joy got burned.

Joy could walk, but with the clumsiness of someone not yet two. While Mother made up the beds, Joy tagged along. I had arranged the tracks of both train sets into one route that snaked across the landing. Then I wound the spring motors on both engines and placed them facing each other across the room. I sat by one engine with my finger on the start lever wondering how I could release both at once and send them headlong into one marvellous crash. Lucky for me, Fred had gone outside; he'd thump me if he caught me crashing his engine.

Maybe Joy could help. Seeing her in the bedroom, I gestured for her to come. She toddled through the doorway, lost her balance, and stumbled toward the Quebec heater, her hands raised to ward off the glowing firebox. We no longer used the safer but inefficient furnace. I tried to call out, "J-J-J . . ." but it jammed in my throat.

Joy screamed. The acrid smell of burning flesh and the shriek hit me with far greater force than I could have mustered with the collision of a thousand tiny engines. I tried to rise, but remained as though stapled to the linoleum. I should have yelled, should have run to head her off, should have—.

Mother rushed into the room, scooped up Joy from where she had fallen at the base of the heater, and rushed downstairs, wailing child in arms.

I pulled myself free and followed Mother, blubbering, "Mommy, I called her . . . I should have . . . I might have . . ."

"Quit your whining," Mother snapped. "Joy's hurt, not you. She's seriously burned her arms, but fortunately not her face. Don't just stand there! Go find your brother. Quickly!"

Only half dressed for outdoors, and still blubbering, I followed the snow-banked path toward the barn and chicken house where I found Fred feeding the chickens. He could make no sense out of my whining and wailing. When he finally understood my words "Joy burned" he dropped the feed pail and ran for the house.

Despite my near hysterical state, I had the sense to clean up the spilled feed before the hens could gorge on it. I returned to the house in time to see Fred leave the farmyard at a full run.

Back in the house Joy's near-hysterical screaming had mellowed to a whimper. Mother spoke, "I've rubbed butter on the burns and bandaged them. Fred's gone to the Johanson's to see if they can take us to the doctor."

Why oh why did adults insist on speaking to me like an adult! I thought I had caused the problem and needed help myself.

The rest of the day passed in a blur. Grandpa came in his '27 Chev. Roads aren't bad," he said, "I think we can get through."

We got to the doctor in jig time. The trip brightened me up; I rarely got to ride in a car. Fred, Grandpa Johanson, and I sat in the tiny waiting room staring at the door into the doctor's inner office. My own experience in that torture chamber a few months previously came back so forcibly, I began to cry.

The doctor, smiling broadly, ushered mother and Joy out, but when he saw me the smile faded. Looking straight at me, he asked, "Are you still blubbering?"

Mother later described the encounter with Dr. Rich. "Joy never complained at all when he fixed her up. But he bawled me out for putting butter on the burns. Worst thing I could have done. Told me I should have applied cold tea; the tannic acid in the tea helps heal the burn."

Joy's burns healed quickly, but for years she would hold her arms up, palms forward, showing the burn marks that ran from wrist to elbow. That stirred mixed feelings in me: guilt because I thought I had caused the accident, and pride that I had such a brave little sister.

Brother, it's cold out!

"You can't go out. Don't ask again," Mother's voice reverberated up the stairs from the kitchen. "As long as you have a fever you stay inside. It's 30 below out there."

I padded to the window, keeping a quilt wound tightly about my preschool body like the robe of an eastern prince. I could see nothing outside. Jack Frost had painted icy pictures that covered each pane. In them I saw lakes and leaves, meadows and mountains, clouds and cascades, all etched in white and grey. I pressed my pudgy hand against one of the clouds until the ice melted in a tiny circle just big enough for my eye.

Through this tiny porthole, I beheld a prairie day in the grip of winter. Snowflakes, turned to tiny icy pellets, angled past the window, some of them striking the glass with the force of tiny hailstones. On the road where it dipped through the coulee, I saw a small van mounted on sleighs and pulled by two black horses.

Breath burst from their nostrils like steam escaping from a railway engine. Even at a distance I could see icicles hanging from their muzzles like spiky beards. I imagined the tinkle of sleigh bells. I pictured children inside a bigger van, and thought, "Next year I'll go to school with the big kids and ride in a van behind a team of horses."

Close to the house, a huge snowdrift ran from the caragana hedge halfway to the barn. I knew the dry wind would harden the snow's surface until a heavy man could walk over its crust. I wanted to run on top of the drift four feet above the ground. I wanted to slide on the hard surface with the wind at my back. I wanted to cut a hole through the crust and hollow out the drift like an igloo or a polar bear's den. I wanted to wrestle with my brother in the soft snow within our den. Tears came as I thought of Fred Junior away all day at school.

"Let me go out!" I demanded.

Mother just ignored me. I'd have to wait for another day.

I survived that winter, but my loneliness made me search for new adventures. I made it right through till spring without getting into real trouble. Then I pulled the biggest misdeed of my short life.

And then, fire!

Folks living in old prairie farmhouses like ours needed matches to keep the place livable. Mom used them to light the wick-type oil lamp in the kitchen, and the Aladdin mantel lamp in the living room. She needed matches to ignite the newspaper under the kindling that started the wood or coal in the kitchen cook stove and the Quebec heaters that warmed the place. She kept matches within reach of all those appliances—and handy to the barn lanterns and emergency candles.

I forget where I picked up the matches that fateful day. Maybe I found them on the brass candle holder, the one that held two inches of white candle. With candle holder in hand, I slipping into my bedroom, looking for a place to put my prohibited toy. The lure of the forbidden overpowered Mom's instructions never to play with matches; so I placed the candle holder on the floor between the twin beds out of sight of anyone who might venture near. To further ensure my security, I closed the door. I lit the match like an old pro—by striking it across the sole of my shoe. I touched it to the candle.

Stretched out on my stomach, I peered into the dancing light for a few moments. But soon bored with the tiny flame, I cast about for better fuel. Retrieving a newspaper, I tore it into small pieces, crunched them up, and placed them around the base of the candle on the brass holder. Carefully, I held a torn piece to the flame and used it to light the others. The yellow and red tongues soon leaped upwards to the height of the beds, then grew smaller as they consumed the paper. I watched, mesmerized, until I heard steps outside the room. In fear and desperation I swept the flaming candle holder under the bed.

"Time for lunch, Stan," Mother said as she stepped into the room. She didn't pause in the doorway, but continued moving forward, her nose twitching as she sniffed the air.

"Have you been playing with fire?" she roared as her 150-pound, five-foot-two frame rounded the end of the bed. In one sweeping movement she threw herself onto her knees, swept me aside with one arm and pushed back the bed with the other. Grabbing the brass candle holder, she smothered the flames with a wet dish towel providence had caused her to bring from the kitchen. Fortunately, the bed had not ignited.

Mother didn't waste any words explaining the dangers of fire; she had done that a hundred times before. She went straight to the seat of the problem and gave me a sound spanking—I made most of the sound! As the seriousness of what I had done registered, I wept and begged Mom not to tell anyone, especially Noel, my hero. He had become an important father figure to me since Pop's illness.

She not only told Noel, but spread the word among the neighbours. I am sure every child for miles around heard a lecture using little Stan Stone as a good illustration of a bad kid. For weeks I could look no one in the face, but I never again played with matches.

Even today, when I remember those flames reaching out for the bedclothes, when I recall that flimsy wooden house, when I realize we had no fire department or smoke alarm and only a cheap fire extinguisher, I thank God. Surely as a child I should have heard the rush of my guardian angel's wings as he sped from the room and down the stairs to summon Mother. Normally she would have simply used her mighty mezzo voice to call me to lunch.

Noel makes a difference

Way back when Pop built the house, he had fashioned a lean-to entrance to protect the kitchen door from the weather. At the lean-to door he had placed a large stone in lieu of steps. That stone connected the yard, indeed the farm and the whole universe, to my life indoors. I often sat there, halfway between two worlds, watching the sky or listening to the birds in the grove that protected the house from west winds. I looked on it as a happy place. Tippy often joined me there—sitting quietly after rooting under my arm from behind and turning his head up to lick my face.

But I also had a sad place; for want of a better name, I call it my wailing post. The old shaft had once anchored the swinging side of a gate. But the gate had long gone and the old pine stake stood barren and alone at the rear or north-west corner of the lean-to; not at all far from my happy place. Only Tippy ever shared my sad place.

I visited that post often in my pre-school days. With one arm wrapped around it, I would whine, and cry, and snivel, and pour out tales of woe. Why did I pick that post as the object of my grief and sorrow? Possibly because it had lost its purpose and stood forlorn and useless, and so I saw it as a fellow traveller on the road to self-pity and misery. More likely it marked a halfway point between the security of the house and the terrors that must surely lurk just beyond in the empty prairie landscape. Whatever the reason, I arrived often to grip its shredded bark, and whine, and howl, and cry out my protests against a cruel and unfair world.

Goodness knows I had plenty to complain about. Rarely did anyone buy me new toys; typically I got used ones at Christmas and birthdays. All my clothes came as hand-me-downs from my older brother and neighbours. I tasted candy only at Christmas and never had spending money on the rare times we visited town. My big brother picked on me, and my father spent most of his time in the hospital.

Then in one magic moment, it all changed. My circumstances didn't alter, if anything they worsened. But my attitude toward them underwent a revolution. My hero, Noel, on an unexpected visit, appeared around the corner as I clung to my snivelling post, sending a mighty howl heavenward.

Noel came to a halt at the sight of this small boy clinging to a post and wailing loudly. This quiet man of few words, but capable of great depth and understanding, stood and stared and gathered his thoughts. He did not know if inward or outward pain had provoked my outburst; indeed, I no longer recall the cause.

Noel reached out and touched me with his voice; men rarely used physical contact to communicate tenderness back then. "Lad," he said quietly, "whatever has hurt you can't be all that bad. Why not save all that crying, and noise, and energy for some time when you really need it? When you really hurt."

I don't know if Noel's unexpected appearance, tender words, or common sense did it, but something at that moment changed me. I won't claim I never again whined or complained about my lot in life, but Noel's intervention meant I did less than I might have.

Shopping

The shops in Gawain filled one block that ran at a right angle to the railroad, with the grain elevators on the far side of the tracks. A two-story hotel and a hardware store anchored the railroad end of the street. A restaurant and another hardware store cum John Deere dealer occupied the other. A variety of diverse shops, including two general dealers, a meat market, a post office, a couple of assorted offices, and a drug store, filled the in-between space along the wide, wooden sidewalks.

Almost every shop had a painted, wooden false front that hid the gable end of its roof. Well, most of them had seen paint at least once in bygone years. All displayed faded signs indicating the proprietor's name and business. For all the world it looked like a scene from a western movie—except for the people.

Few men on the streets of Gawain sported wide-brimmed hats. Most men and boys wore bibbed denim overalls. None had six-guns stuck through wide studded belts, though some young men chose jeans and large-buckled belts.

We shopped at McDermot's general store. Old Scotty McDermot would stand behind the cash drawer that stood on the front end of the long counter that kept customers from the groceries lining the shelves on the wall. When Mom ordered pails of peanut butter, honey, or Roger's corn syrup, he'd retrieve the products from the shelves, place them on the counter, and laboriously write them into a sales book. For some things like oatmeal or bran, he would come in front of the counter and measure them from large drums.

While Mom shopped for groceries, Fred and I would wander the shop, looking at piles of clothing, household products, and school supplies piled on tables filling the centre of the store or packed onto shelves against the far wall. We religiously followed Mother's don't-touch orders, sinning only occasionally by running a hand over a flannel shirt or pair of shiny black boots. Then the call came. "Let's go boys."

We'd dash to Mother's side, grabbing for our favourite food—usually the peanut butter or honey pails. We always hesitated for a moment before hefting the pails; some days Scotty would toss us a piece of licorice, a jawbreaker, or two or three jujubes. Almost every visit to the store brought a plea of some sort to Mother from Fred or me. "Mom, they have some keen boots; I need new boots; can't you get me a pair?"

Always, Mother answered, "No. You know his clothing and boots are too expensive. When you need new things, we'll order them through the Eaton's catalogue."

That always caused me a problem. If Scotty charged too much for his clothing, then no one would buy it because people always bought the cheapest, didn't they? But sometimes I'd check for a favourite item the next time we came to town, only to find it gone; someone had bought it. Didn't other mothers know what my mother knew? That everything is cheaper and better from the catalogue?

The arrival of a new catalogue caused at least a full week of excitement in our house, especially the winter edition with its pages of toys. We'd spend hours studying it, dreaming about new toys, sleds, or skates. We'd make long lists, knowing that with a bit of luck we might get one thing each—if we had enough sense to select from the lower-priced items. Mother didn't treat the catalogue much differently. She'd dream about new curtains or wallpaper, an indoor chemical toilet, or a comfortable chair.

One day Mother ordered a washing machine through the catalogue. It didn't have an electric motor because we had no electricity. It wasn't one of those fancy Beatty washers powered by a gasoline engine either. She actually ordered a kid-powered machine! It had a handle that fastened to a rod on the top of the agitator. Mother would place the lid on the machine after filling it with dirty clothes and hot water from the kitchen stove. She'd then put the handle in place and order Fred or me to start swinging the handle back and forth. Because it took a lot more power, she'd turn the wringer handle herself.

We enjoyed it for the first week!

You could buy almost anything through the catalogue—Mom even ordered new dentures by mail!

Mother had a lower denture. One day while cleaning it, she dropped it, breaking it in two. Initially, she didn't know what to do, what with lack of money and the difficulty of going to Edmonton or Camrose for a fitting and replacement. Then she saw an ad in *The Family Herald*—a dental company in Edmonton would send her a kit to fit her own dentures.

The kit arrived containing a wax form or mouthpiece. Mother heated the wax and bit into it leaving the impression of her gums. She sent that back to the company; they made the new teeth and mailed them back. They fitted perfectly, and she wore them for years.

The Eaton's catalogue, *The Toronto Star Weekly*, and *The Family Herald* kept us in touch with the outside world, but their usefulness didn't end there. We recycled them to the outhouse where they served another vital purpose.

Chapter 3

School daze

Life begins anew

Life continued much the same, with occasional visits to Pop in Ponoka, and with even rarer but volatile visits home on his part. We struggled financially and Mother exchanged letters with the Public Administrator to no avail. But one thing did change. I had my seventh birthday in June and started first grade in September. Now I rode with Fred in the school van and made new friends. I got to carry a black lunch pail with a round top something like a barn roof, and eat in the cloakroom with the other boys.

I'd usually get sandwiches spread with salted beef or pork drippings, or Mom's home-made jam, or even peanut butter. In addition to sandwiches, some kids brought fruit or cake and I'd look on with envy; I sometimes had raw carrots or tomatoes, and occasionally cookies.

The teacher introduced my fellow students and me to the magic of letters and words. Although I warmed quickly to words, I found numbers less friendly.

At times I found other boys even more unfriendly—especially those in the higher grades. "Hey listen to this guy," one ruffian called to his friends as he backed me against an outside wall.

"Hey kid, say it again. What do you call this thing around your neck?" he demanded, pulling on my scarf.

"It's a *scawf*," I said, trying to act defiantly, but with tears beginning.

The circle of older kids pressing around me roared with laughter. "He sure talks funny," my tormentor declaimed to his followers.

"What do you call this?" he said, holding a pocket mirror before me.

I saw the tears on my cheeks and felt my muscles tighten. I wanted to strike out, but I didn't dare, so I meekly answered, "It's a *mirrow*."

Again laughter rippled around the circle. I looked for Fred; Fred would come to my rescue. Then I saw Fred standing just beyond the circle, watching—just watching, but doing nothing! Anger boiled inside me; I ducked low, charged through the crowd, and raced for the door, bawling as I went. No one attempted to stop me, but their laughter followed me inside.

I couldn't know that Fred had faced an even worse initiation in grade one the year before. The bullies had surrounded him in a remote corner of the schoolyard and attacked him verbally: "Your father's in the nut house. Your old man is crazy. They locked up your dad because he's bonkers!"

I guess Fred thought I'd got off easy.

The Van

At least a half dozen school vans picked up country kids and converged on Gawain Consolidated School. Soon after the turn of the century, the province built one-room school houses throughout rural Alberta. One of them had stood on the south-east corner of our farm until 1919 when the school area around Gawain consolidated and built a six room school in Gawain to house grade 1 through 12.

They also built a fleet of horse-drawn vans to transport the kids to town. At first they ran them on steel-rimmed wagon wheels, but later adapted frames and wheels salvaged from Model-T Fords or similar cars. The ride improved greatly with the rubber tires, but the motive force remained at two horsepower.

We spent a lot of time in the vans—anywhere from 30 minutes to two hours each way, depending on how they adjusted the routes. I sometimes think we learned more in the van than we did at school.

One hard lesson stands out almost too clearly. One day on the way home in the van, we entertained each other with solos. I could hardly wait for my turn. My older brother refused his opportunity, passing the imaginary microphone to me. A smarter kid than I would have figured it out; my brother Fred never sang, not around the house and never in public.

With all the kids looking my way, I belted out a verse of *Home on the Range*. Almost as good, I thought, as Wilf Carter.

I was sure our driver, Montana, would like it—he wore cowboy boots and hat and thought himself more cowboy than a farmer.

Nobody said a word. The silence became so thick, I thought I had become deaf. Then Montana, spoke, "I guess it was alright Stan, but you can't carry a tune. You couldn't carry a tune in a feedbag. Don't ever again sing in public."

The kids laughed, including Fred.

When the van dropped us off at our gate five minutes later, I outran Fred to the house. Bursting into the kitchen, I yelled, "Mom, Montana says I can't sing. He says I can't carry a tune."

Mother never told a lie. Without turning to me from the kitchen table and with her mixing spoon rattling like a machine gun against the big mixing bowl, she spoke. "You can't carry a tune. Neither can your father nor brother. I've tried to teach you, but I guess you inherited Pop's tin ear."

Fear

The contraption parked near the outdoor rink behind the school rested on the chassis of a farm wagon. About the length of a car, flat on top and half-cylindrical underneath, it could have been a boat. An open hatch at one end made me think *submarine*. One of my more knowledgeable, grade-one pals explained, "It's a water tank; they use it to bring water from the well to flood the ice rink in winter."

At recess time I joined the gang that went to explore the tank; it might prove a useful diversion for us prairie kids who experienced few novelties in our isolated lives. As I approached, three bigger boys scrambled from the hatch and jumped to the ground. Not normally a leader, I saw my chance and climbed the wagon tongue, pulled myself to the top of the oddity, and dropped in through the hatch.

On hands and knees, I began moving slowly toward the back. I hadn't counted on four other boys following and blocking my escape. As the others cut off most of the light and some of the air, my body tensed, I could breath only in short gasps, and I began to scream. Kids often react slowly to events outside their experience; by the time they let me out, sweat soaked my clothes and tremors racked my body. I had experienced my first attack of uncontrollable fear, of terror.

Okay, I have never considered myself a brave person. But on the other hand, how can anyone ever act with true courage until he or she has first faced crippling fear?

A dangerous toboggan ride

Just before Christmas during the year that I began school, Pop came home for a visit from the hospital. He didn't get home often, so excitement ran high at our house. Before they would release Pop into Mother's care, she had to promise not to let him get excited or overstressed.

"Why don't you take the kids tobogganing?" Mom asked Pop.

Pop agreed. We bundled up with not much more than our eyes and noses exposed. Pop pulled Joy on the toboggan. Fred and I frolicked along behind with Tippy, our unbelievable cross between a collie and a dachshund, yapping at our heels. We went down through the gulley, up the steep coulee hill, and positioned the toboggan at the top.

A dry wind blew ice pellets and fine snow horizontally. In that kind of prairie weather a hard crust forms on the snow, hard enough that day to support Pop's weight. We had a toboggan made from a long steel advertising sign turned up at the end—it said Firestone on the underside. Pop sat on the front, my brother next, then me, and then Joy. Tippy refused to join us. My hands and feet already felt half frozen; given the chance, I'd have gone home right then.

When we started propelling ourselves forward, Joy fell off, so Pop moved her up front where he could hold her, and we started off again.

Pop gave a push with his hands and off we flew at a tremendous speed. Now I really wished I had stayed home. Near the bottom of the hill our heavy and heavily-laden craft broke through the crust of the snow. Large icy pieces shot over the front and bounced off Pop; some of it even struck my arms and shoulders. But Joy took the worst of it right in the face.

Blood oozed from a half dozen small cuts on Joy's face and

mingled with her tears. Pop scooped her up and ran for the house while we followed along with the toboggan. So much for not letting him get excited or stressed. I had never heard Mother and Pop argue, but they came dangerously close that day.

Mom must have talked to someone, because the story soon spread all over the neighbourhood. Tongues prattled and heads wagged. I overheard statements like:

"Have you heard how Fred Stone injured his little girl?"

"The poor man has a mental problem; they should keep him in Ponoka."

"But he seemed well at the time—I think he just used bad judgment."

"Well whatever, the man is crazy you know."

I didn't like them talking about my Pop like that. So we had an accident on the toboggan, so what? I knew all about Pop's illness, but I didn't need to hear anyone calling him crazy.

Death

It must have happened during that first year of school, soon after Eric had bought a tiny red Farmall tractor. The cute little thing looked more suited to working a garden plot than a large Alberta farm, but in those war years anything that would reduce the drudgery and lower the dependency on horses made farmers happy.

Strangely, I don't remember it as a dust-caked, work-saving machine. I think of it as an omen, as a herald of bad news. Late one afternoon, the tiny red machine with Eric at the wheel turned from Grandpa Johanson's lane and raced along the road. It followed that dirt byway through the coulee and up the bank in front of our place. It fairly flew past our gate and out of sight along the road. We had never seen a farm tractor move so quickly. Neither had we ever known the typically easy-going Eric in such a hurry to get somewhere.

For the rest of the day and evening, we wondered where Eric had gone so quickly. It occurs to me only as I write these words, that Eric, a mechanically astute fellow, must have disabled the tractor's governor to make it move so quickly.

Coming home in the school van the following day, Montana said to one of the older kids sitting toward the rear, "Did you hear that Old Man Johanson died yesterday?"

Every kid in the van looked up, startled.

My chest and stomach knotted; it took a full minute before I could speak. "No, Grandpa can't be dead. He isn't dead."

Even though I knew Grandpa couldn't have died, I began crying, keeping it up until the van stopped at our gate. Fred sat in silence, shocked by the announcement of the death, and ashamed of his crybaby brother. Whimpering, I ran all the way to the house. Bursting in, I forced words between broken sobs, "Mommy, Montana said Grandpa died, but it's not true."

But it was true; a neighbour had brought the news to mother earlier in the day. Feeling the loss herself, Mother tried to comfort us and told us the story. When Grandpa didn't return home with a wagon load of grain as planned, Grandma asked Eric to look for him. Grandpa, feeling ill, had stretched out on the wheat with his head resting on the grain scoop. Instead of returning home as many teams would have done, they stopped at the roadside. Eric found him dead from a heart attack.

Because this was my first encounter with death, and because the culture of the time did not permit us to attend the funeral, a little red tractor travelling dangerously fast on a rutted dirt road forever remains imprinted on my soul as a symbol or harbinger of death.

Miss Stryker

True, sometimes I had rough times in the van. But things at school didn't always go well either.

Whack! Swoosh-whack! Swoosh-kawack!

Each time the strap fell on my palm, the grade-2 teacher increased the velocity. She usually doled out three good ones, although if her strength or anger had peaked, she'd not stop under six. Back then, the strap solved most classroom problems for the teacher—if not the student.

Miss Ima Stryker's confused knowledge of anatomy led her to believe that pain in my hand would stimulate my brain. Again, contrary to specific instructions, I had copied incorrectly from the board, mixing up letters and transposing numbers. My frustration in not being able to do what others did so easily triggered behavioral problems, which further incensed the teacher—who obviously had major problems of her own.

Miss Stryker marched me to the cloakroom, strap in hand, when I transposed the numbers in an arithmetic test and got all the answers wrong. When in frustration I asked a question of the child beside me because I had misread a word in my reader, Miss Stryker ordered me to the cloakroom. When my frustration at continually misinterpreting written work boiled over and I hurled a pencil to the floor or let out a burst of verbal anguish, Miss Stryker reached for the strap.

Long before the end of the year, she dispensed with the privacy of the cloakroom and ordered me to the front of the room. Sometimes I simply stood at my desk and held out my hand. If I cried too hard, or didn't cry at all, she gave me extra whacks. One Friday afternoon as we piled into the school van, Bert whacked me across the back and said, "Wow, you had a great week. You got the strap only once!"

Bert, a big heavy kid, about Fred's age, and always friendly to Fred and me, meant well. I could usually count on him as a pal, although we rarely agreed on anything.

Somehow I managed to keep the teacher's abuse from Mother. On rare occasions when my frustrations triggered a particularly naughty outburst, Fred would tell her. "Stan got strapped today for hitting Vivian because she laughed at him."

That usually resulted in further punishment at home. Mother had a bigger strap that she applied directly to the seat of the problem. She'd deliver a lecture with it, "If the teacher strapped you (whack), she had a good reason (whack). Don't you ever hit a girl again (whack)."

I hadn't taken any full scribblers home during the school year, but had let them pile up in my desk. How could I let Mother see the teacher's comments? Surely that would trigger more wrath. At the end of the school year, I had no option; Mother would expect to see them. But even worse, my report card bore the inscription: "Stanley Stone has failed his year and must repeat grade 2."

I placed the report card and books in front of Mother and waited for the explosion. As she read the report card, her face screwed up into a frown. When she leafed from page to page and scribbler to scribbler, the frown became as black as a prairie dust storm. On one page after another, she read the teacher's comments: Why don't you write what's written on the blackboard?

Then she exploded. "What kind of an idiot do you have for a teacher? Why didn't she tell me you were having trouble seeing."

Given that information Mother made a decision based on her understanding of the facts. If I couldn't read the blackboard, I obviously needed glasses. That summer a travelling optometrist came to Gawain. Mother managed to find the $10 for the test and glasses. When I returned to grade 2 in September, I went as "four eyes," although I wore them only in class. The next year I moved close to the top of the class and the strapping ceased, but it had nothing to do with the glasses and much to do with a new teacher.

I really didn't have a major problem. Today, educators would describe it as a learning disability or dyslexia, and prescribe a little more patience and personal assistance. Of course, back then a teacher at Gawain Consolidated didn't have much time for individual students, not with three grades and about 30 students in one classroom. She didn't have much education either—grade12 and one year of normal school or teacher's college.

People don't grow out of learning disabilities. I learned to cope with mine.

The glasses? Two years later Mother threw them out when another optometrist declared them worthless, nothing but window glass.

Dog meat

The summer between my first and second try at grade two, I learned a lesson that had nothing to do with school. Few kids can accurately judge the consequences of their actions. I certainly couldn't on that glorious summer day when Mother commanded, "Run out to Aunt

Dolly and Noel's rig and get our copy of *The Star Weekly*. They brought it from town."

I ran outside while she chatted with Noel and Aunt Dolly.

As I scooted across the brown prairie grass toward the horse and buggy, Tippy yapped at my heels. I climbed the back of the buggy, pulled open a large cardboard carton, and saw the Star atop a parcel of waxed brown paper—the kind butchers used. I didn't give the parcel a second thought—I had discovered that my new reading skills gave me access to parts of the newspaper. So with *The Star* in my hands, I sped back to the house.

I didn't notice that Tippy stayed by the rig instead of racing along with me. I got the bad news that evening. It seems that Noel and Aunt Dolly missed the roast only when they arrived home and removed the box from the buggy. After chores that evening, they retraced their journey and found the torn waxed paper in our yard. Tippy, with bursting tummy, could barely bark a greeting. No one could figure how the short-legged thief got into the buggy, but I paid for leaving the box open.

I didn't get thumped for that one. Mother decreed that I should repay Noel for the roast, the sum of $1.27! That proved a major challenge; in a good month Mother might find five or ten cents each as an allowance for Fred and me. Should I ask Noel or Willie to let me help with chores for a few cents? Or could I snare gophers for the one-cent bounty paid for each gopher tail? Somehow I paid it off by the following spring!

That taught me a basic lesson in farm life: the principle of limited access—keep lids on boxes, shut gates in fences, and close doors into buildings to control who or what can enter. Even then I had a fair amount of responsibility, so I should have known better. As for Tippy, he never got another roast for dinner.

The difficult years

During these difficult years Fred and I never realized that some people in the world would consider us dirt poor. In fact, apart from the garden plot, coulee, and farm buildings, we had no economic access to the 320 acres of land. Mother did manage to keep an animal or two in the barn, feeding them from whatever food nature provided or what she could scrounge from helpful neighbours. Keeping chickens proved no problem; we could feed them from grain that leaked from the farm wagons and granaries of those to whom the public administrator had leased the land.

We'd always raised chickens. Either the brood hens sat on the eggs, hatched, and raised chicks in the normal fashion, or Mother took over the process with an incubator. That device used an oil lamp to keep the eggs warm. Excitement for us kids peaked when tiny beaks pecked through the shell and the little yellow balls of fluff broke free.

We'd watch the little creatures grow and begin to sprout feathers. In a few weeks Mom would set them free to join their bigger relatives in the barnyard and establish a position in the pecking order of chicken culture. Often we'd make a pet of one so it would run to greet us when we approached.

The chicken house became my domain. Mother trusted me to feed them, open the chicken house door in the morning to let them out, and close it at night to stop skunks and coyotes from entering. That practice annoyed the skunks and coyotes, but it certainly pleased the chickens.

Throughout that time I really liked chickens. But sometimes a virus would strike and kill many of the young—or they would turn cannibal and eat each other. At that point I'd cry.

Although I often made pets of them, all of us ate chicken. Our menu went something like this: Sunday, roast chicken; Monday, cold chicken; Tuesday, scrambled eggs; Wednesday, fried chicken; Thursday, fried eggs; Friday . . . well you get the idea. Mother had dozens of chicken recipes. She would stew the scrawny, tough old hens on the stove top for hours.

I began to turn against chicken.

Mom also raised turkeys. These she sold for cash or traded to the butcher for other meat, so we rarely ate them. They generally ran loose around the farm, so coyotes and disease often cut into our profits.

Most lessees who worked our fields acted kindly toward us, on occasion dropping off feed and grain. But Fred and I resented some. It bothered us to see strangers on Pop's land, on our land. We glared at them as they passed through our yard; those with the John Deere and Massey Harris tractors seemed most arrogant. Others with horse-drawn implements seemed more friendly, often asking us to ride along for a few turns around the fields.

We'd tell them, "Pop always farmed with horses," even though that took place long before our time. Mom had told us all about the great teams Pop drove. She also told us that he had bought the first John Deere tractor to come into the Gawain district. He used it only for pulling stumps, breaking new land, and threshing—preferring to use horses for most farm work. Pop had experienced great success, eventually extending his holdings to many sections. He sold most of the land in the 1920s to tour the world.

Now these strangers dared come onto our land with their fancy machines and pay the public administrator, not us, for the privilege.

A real threshing

Threshing brought high excitement, no matter who had leased the land. Most often two or three farmers would band together to create their own threshing crew, using a small thresher and two or three hayracks. They would move at a fairly leisurely pace to thresh the crops only on their own farms, eating in each-others homes as the work progressed from farm to farm.

The biggest crews arrived with a larger thresher, a big tractor, a bunk house, a cook house, and a crew of hired men driving a whole squadron of hayracks. They'd often arrive on a farm, complete the threshing and move on in two days. Our family friend, Al Nixon, ran an operation like that.

The shortage of gasoline brought on by the war hampered Al's threshing enterprise. He solved it by resurrecting his huge Rumley tractor. This ancient machine that burned heavy oil instead of gasoline hadn't been out of his storage shed for two decades. One sunny August day I saw it rolling onto our south field, towing a fuel wagon, a wheeled bunk house, a cook house, and a train of hay racks. Its stack, puffing bursts of black smoke, stood as tall as a house. A huge flywheel spun at its side, and great metal wheels, taller than a man, dug into the field, dragging the train along at walking speed. Al stood on the engine's footboard behind a large steering wheel and surrounded by great levers.

"Fred, Fred," I yelled. "Come and see the steam engine."

Fred and I soon learned it wasn't really a steam engine, but that didn't quench our enthusiasm; we made plans to watch it in action. At eight the following morning we found it set up and operating alongside the slough in our west field. The spout of the thresher spewed straw onto the low willow bushes by the slough; another smaller spout poured grain into a waiting wagon; a farmhand atop a massive load of bundles pitched them into the waiting maw of the wonderful threshing machine.

We parked ourselves with our backs against a wagon wheel in a safe place near the engine and threshing machine. We thrilled at the steady beat of the huge Rumley engine, the thunderous shaking of the thresher, and the slapping and hiss of the great belt that transferred the power from the engine's pulley to the threshing machine. The belt determined our field of safety; should it break it might lash out like a whip in the hand of a giant, striking down anyone near.

Al Nixon, shirt soaked in sweat, dashed from the engine to thresher, applying belt dressing to the drive belt and to the smaller belts that whirred away on the side of the thresher. The little belts drove all the internal shakers that separated the grain from the straw and chaff. Suddenly a metallic crunch reached our ears over the general din. The thresher seemed to arc its back like an angry cat, then cease its shaking. Two small belts flew from its side, but the roar of the engine and the swish of the great belt continued, unaffected by the threshing machine's distress.

With a frenzy of lever pulling, Al brought all action to a halt. He inspected the feed chute that carried the bundles into the machine, then removed a panel and crawled inside. We saw his feet and legs hanging out the opened access that led to the bowels of the machine; they swung up and down as he worked inside. The farmhand who a moment before had been using a pitchfork to toss bundle after bundle into the chute, now stood atop his load, hands on hips, face glowing bright red.

Al wiggled out of the machine, stood erect on top of it, turned toward the red-faced farmhand, and heaved the broken halves of a pitchfork to the ground. Whatever he said to the hapless farmhand, he buried in the midst of a stream of curses. Fred and I learned a few new words we'd never dare use. Within minutes Al closed the opened panel, replaced the belts, and set everything in motion. The farmhand continued pitching in the bundles with a borrowed pitchfork.

All morning the action continued. As one hayrack emptied its load into the hungry machine another took its place. The emptied rack headed back into the field for another load, the horses knowing to follow the rows of stooked grain, stopping long enough for the farmhand to pitch the bundles on. When the load towered as high as the man could reach with a pitchfork, the rack returned to join the queue to unload.

When the action stopped for lunch, we raced home to eat quickly and return. We found Al still on site, adjusting his equipment, climbing over the thresher, pumping grease into dozens of fittings, and refuelling the engine.

We parked ourselves against the wagon wheel, Al restarted the machinery, and the parade of hayracks began again. The pile of straw grew as big as a barn and wagonload after wagonload of grain left for the grain elevator or temporary storage in a granary.

Fred and I looked at the huge straw stack, then grinned at each other. We knew that the weight of the straw on the willows would bend them low, creating passageways under the stack. Next week we'd crawl into them, exploring the straw caves before skunks and other wild critters registered their claim.

Allowances and gophers

Way back when Pop selected the site for the homestead buildings, the surveyors hadn't yet marked out the road allowances. He positioned the house facing east near the coulee bank overlooking a gully that entered the coulee. He thought the road would pass through the gully a few yards in front of the house, but the surveyor placed it another 200 yards to the east. This left a few acres of land in front of the house, including the gully, that remained as virgin prairie.

Each spring the bank of the gully nearest the house turned bright purple as millions of crocuses burst through the soil. Gophers, little rodents known correctly as Richardson's Ground Squirrels, also liked the hillsides. Their holes or burrows honeycombed all areas that had never seen the plow—roadsides, yards, and pastures—where a careless farm animal might step into them and break a leg.

You must remember that only a half century earlier, settlers had broken the soil, driven out most predatory animals, and declared war on all varmints and vermin that made farming difficult. We saw driving gopher colonies from our hillsides as a continuation of the process started by our ancestors. We also saw it as a means to earn some money.

Although the garden, henhouse, and barn provided most of our food, we needed cash for extras. Mother often worked at odd tasks to earn money, but as kids we wanted things she couldn't provide. So we trapped gophers.

The government paid one or two cents for each tail sent to the appropriate office. We would spend whole days setting traps, or waiting quietly at the exit hole with a club or snare. Often we'd speed the process by pouring water into the critters' holes and dispatching them when they tried to escape. On a good day we might get 15 gophers, snip off their tails and save them in an old tobacco tin.

Unfortunately, we rarely got paid for the tails we gathered. By the time we figured out where to send them, they'd smell so bad Mother would order us to throw them out.

In another attempt to make money during the winters, Fred set up trap lines to catch weasels and rabbits whose animal runs crisscrossed the coulee bottom and banks. I recall him stretching up to a half dozen pelts on boards awaiting delivery to a fur-trader.

Storytelling

In grade two, the second time around, we had a sharing time almost every day. I didn't join in at the beginning of the year, but waited until I got the hang of things. A few weeks into the year, my contributions began as my fertile imagination created adventures and wild high jinks. I clearly recall my fellow classmates, especially those who lived in town, becoming spellbound at my adventures on our isolated farm. I remember also the teacher's concerned frown.

However, my career as a master storyteller would soon end. At about Christmas time, a teacher quit, prompting the reorganizing of the lower grades. As it happened, my brother's class doubled up with mine.

That day at sharing time a classmate tossed me a knowing look and said to the entire room, "Stan didn't have a story today."

Only then did I realize I hadn't been getting away with it. Years passed before I regained the nerve to speak in public again.

My interest in storytelling changed from creator to consumer as my reading skills improved. The arrival of *The Star Weekly* (often days late via a neighbour) fired my passion for stories. Lying on my stomach on the living room floor, I worked through the misadventures of Greg Clark and Jimmy Frise—and despite my own story-telling experience, I believed every word!

Toward the end of that school year, I did have an exciting tale to share—a true story.

Runaway!

On the day in question, a brilliant yellow sun hammered down, driving all moisture from the packed dirt of the narrow road. During the last rain, before the beginning of the hot spell, a Model-A Ford had plowed deep ruts into the road. The ruts told the story—the driver had fought the wheel as the car skidded from side to side, leaving evidence of its passage etched deeply into the road's now rock-hard surface.

Our spirited team of matched bays, heads held high and necks arched, pulled against the driver's grip on the reins and weaved from side to side following the uncertain track. Without a signal from the driver the horses straddled the right rut so the wheels of the school van rode on the smoothest portion of the road.

The green van had a narrow door at the rear for entry and another at the front, opening at the horses' rumps and over the wagon tongue. Padded benches along each side could hold six or eight kids with knees bumping those of as many kids on the opposite bench.

We'd just left a year-end party with only two days of school remaining. So when eight of us piled into the door at the rear of the van, most carried our usual books and lunch buckets, but we also had bags of peanuts and candy.

Montana sat on the front end of the left bench holding the reins that fed out through a slot in the front door. That day he had rolled up the canvas curtains on each side of the van so we had a panoramic view of the countryside through rusted fly screening. As long as the driver and horses avoided the ruts, the van swayed gently but ran smoothly on its rubber tires.

We all bubbled with excitement, eating peanuts and candy as the horses drew us briskly through miles of cultivated prairie interspersed with patches of brush surrounding sloughs. In a surprise sense of comradeship, we contributed our peanuts to one pile on a clear section of seat between Orton and Reggie, but all kept an eye on Reggie so he wouldn't grab more than his share. At age 10, Reggie was little brother to 15 year-old Orton Stone. Orton had the build of a jockey and looked much like his dad, my half-brother Willie. Reggie looked more like Fred—large framed and powerful.

Orton hoped to quit school next year, but Reggie found himself stranded in third grade. Today, experts would say he had learning disabilities. But in 1942 educators just shrugged him off.

Brother Fred, Jack—a grade-niner—and three girls of assorted ages completed the count of passengers.

Orton, seated opposite Montana, begged, "Let me drive."

"Not a chance," said Montana. "They'd get away on you."

But he finally weakened and turned over the reins. Within moments Orton let the leather straps slip from his sweaty hands and through the slot. We all gasped as they disappeared and the team, feeling a sense of freedom, broke into a full gallop. The van raced along with a great rooster tail of dust rising behind, just like a scene from a western movie.

Montana pushed open the front door and helplessly watched the reins dragging between the horses on the dirt road. When the road dipped down into a coulee—actually the same coulee that intersected our farm a few miles on—we all knew a difficult situation had suddenly turned dangerous. As the horses shifted into overdrive, the van rocked treacherously, its wheels bouncing in and out of the ruts. Jack, seated at the rear door yelled, "Jump! Jump backwards and hit the ground running."

We jumped. I landed on the run but, clumsy then as now, fell forward and slid for ten feet on my face and stomach. No worse for wear, we watched the van alternately bounce clear of its running gear, then fall back into place as it continued its wild journey. In horror we realized Reggie had stayed inside the speeding, swaying vehicle.

Still aboard, our cowboy driver stepped through the van's narrow front door and placed one foot on the bouncing wagon tongue. The wind ripped the Stetson from his head and sent it spiralling high in the air. Releasing his grip on the doorposts, he threw himself forward, each hand grabbing the harness straps of a horse. After two steps along the tongue, he leaped onto Star's back and scooped up the reins where they passed through guide loops. Roy Rogers or Hopalong Cassidy couldn't have done better.

We ran the quarter mile to the stopped rig, picked up the hat along the way, and piled back in. Reggie, complete with a smug look and a bulging tummy, and seated exactly where we left him, popped the last of the peanuts into his mouth.

Although none received injuries beyond minor bruises and scrapes, our little adventure had plenty of political fallout. The school board blistered the farmer who held the contract to run the van, the farmer fired Montana, and Montana didn't speak to Orton for three months.

Shotguns

Pop had cleverly built the barn into the bank of the coulee. The south side had an entrance directly to the hayloft through the angled side of the gambrel roof. On the north, the windowless and doorless side, the bank dropped steeply away to the coulee bottom. At the narrow west end a path went part way down the hill to a flat area giving access to the barn through a sliding door at the main level. The cows entered here. Projecting from this end, Pop had built a high wall to protect the door from north winds attacking over the coulee. It made a perfect play area for us as kids, hiding us behind the brow of the coulee bank from watchers at the house on the south side, and from the view of neighbours across the coulee to the north. During windy weather, typical of most days on the prairies, it provided us with a tiny sheltered canyon.

For reasons I don't fully understand, I fondly remember this play area as a hideaway. One day as we looked over the wall, we saw two men with shotguns entering our coulee from the far side. We knew what they wanted. Three large ponds covered much of the coulee bottom as it passed through our farm. Bulrushes surrounded the ponds, but a properly booted hunter could approach close enough to scare up the ducks and pick them off as they lifted from the water.

With Pop away at the hospital, Fred and I felt responsible for the farm; and we knew the hunters had not asked permission to enter our property. I'm not sure who got the idea first, but we began scrambling around for rocks, smooth prairie stones of about a pound each. Then we waited for the hunters to get nearer the bulrushes.

The moment the interlopers reached the rushes, we began heaving the rocks against the extended wall. It acted like a great sounding board so reverberations about as loud as shotgun blasts rolled down into the coulee scaring every duck into the air. It caught the hunters off guard; before they could feed shells into their guns, the ducks had reached a safe altitude.

At that point we jumped from behind the wall and with our prepubescent squeaky voices yelled at the hunters to get off our property.

We sat on the bank, high enough to watch the hunters leave—and to hear their curses. As they drove away to the north, we talked about the future, how one day as grown men we could properly defend our property. As the sun beat down on us, we sprawled on the grass and wondered what the farm would look like in the year 2000.

Never very good at arithmetic, I said, "My gosh, by then I'll be . . ." When I ran out of fingers and toes, I said, "old!"

"I'll be 68," Fred said.

Often after that, I would return to that spot and, with a boy's vivid imagination, wonder about the future and the year with the magical number, the year 2000.

Fear again

The ducks vanished from the coulee ponds and autumn slowly dissolved into winter. I greeted the cold, white season with mixed feelings—I both feared and loved it.

"Stan, did you shut up the chicken house?" Mom asked one dark winter night.

I had forgotten. The cold shivers of dread that crawled up my spine created more discomfort than the snowball my brother Fred had stuffed down my shirt the previous day. I had reason to feel dread. I had seen the damage a coyote can do in a chicken coop: feathers, blood, and dead bodies strewn across the floor; survivors clinging in terror to the highest perch.

"No, Mom," I said, pulling on my parka. "I'll go now."

But then the next wave of icy terror hit me. Darkness had descended outside; a thick blanket of cloud smothered every glimmer from stars, moon, and northern lights. I stepped through the doorway and listened to the aloof stillness of the prairie night. I could see nothing but a yellow flicker on the snow where the light from the oil lamp in the kitchen filtered through a frost-caked window pane. Listening more carefully, I could hear the muffled "thump, huff-huff, thump, huff-huff" of a pump engine running on the neighbour's farm a mile away. Encouraged by that friendly sound I crept further into the dark.

An unexpected coyote howl split the night. It started low, like the yap of a friendly dog, then raised in pitch and power until it rattled my bones. I fell back into the house and kicked the door shut. With quivering hands, I retrieved a hurricane lantern from the porch and took it to Mother. “Mom, light it please,” I begged. “Maybe Fred can . . .,” I started.

She saw my trembling fists and pleading face. Striking a match, she lit the lantern and said, “No, it’s your job. You forgot to do it earlier. The coyote won’t come near you carrying the lantern. Anyway, there’s no record of a coyote attacking a man. Now get down there before it gets into the chicken house.”

Mother dispensed tough love long before the term became popular. I stole into the night thinking, “Coyotes don’t attack men, but what about little kids?”

At the edge of the house I paused, stood in a pool of yellow lantern light on white snow, and considered the 75 inky yards between me and my task. The pump engine had stopped. My imagination took over—I could hear the patter of paws on the hard crust of snow and hot breath expelled in bursts past a lolling tongue and salivating jaw. I ran for the chicken coop, the pool of yellow light swaying along with me. After looking inside to see the chickens huddled together, undisturbed, I closed and fastened the door. Then I rushed back to the house in record time, my shield of protecting light racing along with me.

I had beaten my fear. But only barely!

Mother takes a stand

One Monday morning at 6:20, I sat staring into virtual blackness from the arm of a stuffed chair in the front room. Every minute or two I’d breath on the glass to push back the frost to create a peephole. No starlight or moonlight reached the earth through snow-laden clouds. It hadn’t yet begun snowing, so I could see a pinprick of light at the Johanson farm—an oil lamp, peering at me from a window almost a mile away. I wore my heaviest winter coat—not yet buttoned—boots, and mittens, and clutched my lunch bucket under my arm.

Then I saw it—another pinpoint of light, no bigger than a small star's twinkle about a half mile into the blackness and almost in line with the Johanson light. I set down my lunch pail, began buttoning my coat, and yelled, "The van is coming. I saw the signal from his flashlight."

Running at full tilt, I reached the back door at the same moment Fred came scooting out of the kitchen; he skillfully blocked me so I crashed into the wall. "Get your lunch pail, Numbskull," he yelled as he vanished into the blackness.

Shaken by my collision with the wall and afraid of being left behind, I burst into tears. Mother retrieved my lunch pail, wiped my salty cheeks on her apron, and hurried me out the door with the words, "This is ridiculous! Expecting kids to leave at this time of the morning."

I fell three times in the near blackness. When I reached the gate in the coulee bottom, the van had turned around for its long northern loop of eleven miles to Gawain. Fred had climbed on board at least a minute before I stumbled in and dissolved into tears.

About half way to school, as it began to get light, I retrieved a scribbler from my lunch bucket, wiped the jam off, and began reviewing my sums for an arithmetic test. Many of us did our homework in the van—last week I'd caught it from the teacher for sloppy writing. When I explained that I had done it in the van, she told me to do it at home. When I told her I had to eat, do the chores, and go to bed at home, she rapped me with the pointer for insolence.

Twelve hours later, we returned home in darkness after a full day of school and over four hours in the van. We no sooner had our coats off than Mother made an announcement, "We are going on strike! I've written a note to the school board. Fred, I want you to deliver it to Mr. Harrison at his shop tomorrow."

Mom laid out the letter so we could see it. Fred read it aloud.

Mr. George Harrison,
Chairman of the School Board,
Gawain Consolidated School.

Dear Mr. Harrison,
My boys leave for school before light in the morning and

arrive home after dark. They travel over two hours each way on a van route of eleven miles. When the boys get home, they have time only to eat and sleep. This seems ridiculous to me when the Roseville school van passes our gate a 8:15 a.m. and goes three and a half miles directly to Gawain.

Please arrange for them to travel on the Roseville van. If I have not received your agreement by Friday coming, I will keep the children home from school the following week.

Yours truly,
Harriet Stone

Fred delivered the letter the next day. On Thursday his teacher gave him a sealed envelope addressed to Mrs. Harriet Stone. We sat around the kitchen table while Mother opened and read it.

Dear Mrs. Stone,
I have discussed your suggestion with my fellow trustees. Recognizing the need for haste, I have sent this missive by your son's hand.

The Roseville School District pays Gawain Consolidated for the privilege of sending their pupils to us. They operate their own van, and hence we have no control over it. Therefore, we are unable to accept your suggestion.

You must realize you will subject yourself to prosecution if you keep your children home from school.

Yours truly,
George Harrison
for the Gawain Consolidated School Board

"What is prosecution?" I asked.

"It means they would send the police," Fred said.

Regardless of the potential consequences, Mother sent notes by Fred's "hand" to Mr. Harrison, our teachers, and the van driver. On Monday morning we stayed home.

On strike!

Fred had cut a panel out of a corrugated box and tacked it on the end of a slat borrowed from Mom's kindling box. Using a red crayon, he had written the word *strike* across it. Now he paraded it up and down the kitchen. "Strike! We're on strike," he said.

"What's a strike?" I asked.

Mother, busy wiping down the table, answered, "It's when you refuse to work because you believe the boss has treated you badly."

"But Mom, we don't work!"

Fred chose to straighten me out, "We work at school, and we ain't going back until they put us on the other van."

Mother corrected Fred, "*Aren't* going back to school."

"Aren't," echoed Fred.

She ended her task and sat down, "I went on strike once, and nearly got myself shot for my efforts."

We stared at her. Fred dropped his sign and said, "Tell us about it."

Mom cupped her chin in her hands and placed her elbows on the table—a real no-no if we'd been eating at the time. "In the army," she said. "I joined the WAACs to cook. They stationed us in a camp in France cooking for the boys going up the line. Then one day the officer came to tell us—six of us girls—that we had been transferred to the officers' mess to serve food and drinks.

"All six said no. We went to our barracks and refused to work. We told the commanding officer we had signed up to cook, not to serve officers. He told us he could have us shot for refusing orders. We said, 'Go ahead and shoot us. Just see what the people think of that—the British army shooting women.'"

Fred interrupted, "Why didn't you want to work in the officers' mess?"

I didn't know what a mess was, but I was sure I wouldn't want to work there either.

"You wouldn't understand. Some of the papers in London had said the army sent the women to war as a convenience for the men. We thought working in the mess would further that rumour. And no way did we intend to expose ourselves to the lewd comments and leers of the officers."

Mom had used more words I didn't understand. I'd heard of a toilet called a *convenience*, but what did she mean?

"We stayed off work for three days while the commanding officer continued his threats. Then five of the girls gave up and went to work in the mess. I stayed away alone for two more days. Then they sent me a note telling me to return to the kitchen. People do that; when they can't face you and admit that you are right, they send a note."

"But Mom, they might have shot you," said Fred.

Mother nodded slowly, "Yes, but when it involves a moral principle, you must take a stand regardless of the consequences. On another occasion, I nearly got into trouble. Queen Mary came over to inspect us. They lined us all up on the parade square and told us what a great job we had done, then handed out new badges that said QMAAC instead of WAAC—that stood for Queen Mary's Army Auxiliary Corp.

"I got really mad! Now that we had proven ourselves after all the bad rumours, she decided to give us her name. She should have given us that kind of support when we first went to France. I threw the new badge in the mud and wore the old one for the duration."

Wow! Nobody, not even the Queen, could scare my mother!

On the third day of our strike, Mother got another note—the school van waited at our gate while one of the kids ran it to the house. It said simply:

> Mrs. Stone,
> Please have the boys at the gate at 8:15 a.m. tomorrow to meet the Roseville van.
> G. Harrison

Skating

We didn't worry about the thickness of the ice, not even on the biggest pond in our coulee bottom. During most winters it extended right down to the black prairie muck. Nobody had a better natural skating rink for miles around. Even the Chinook winds that rushed in from the mountains each January did little to thin the ice.

With the help of neighbours, we scraped and shovelled snow until we had cleared an area about half the size of a typical skating rink. I said with the help of neighbours, but they did most of the work. I had neither the physique nor the energy to move much snow.

Things got interesting when the gang arrived on the designated night: grandpas with strap-on skates they had brought from Europe; teenagers with hockey sticks and pucks; little kids with bob skates; and moms and dads who chose to tend the bonfire and hand out hot chocolate. Of course I pulled on my skates—the ones two sizes too big with canvas sides. I couldn't really skate; I'd run on the sides of my feet, then jump up on the blades and coast across the ice. I could neither stop nor change directions.

Orton put together a human whip line. He anchored the end of a line of six to ten kids, each a little smaller progressing toward the end of the whip. With everyone facing the same direction and hands locked together, Orton began skating in tight circles forcing each one in the whip to skate in progressively larger circles at proportionately higher speeds. The littlest kid at the outside found himself moving at highway speeds. Being a trusting soul, I fell for it!

Suddenly Orton dug in his skates, cracking the whip with such force it broke, sending those on the outside hurtling across the ice. All eyes watched the little guy on the very end—well the one who started out on the end! He broke free and rocketed toward the snow piled against the bulrushes. Everyone saw his funny canvas skates and noticed his ankles wobbling without support. Those nearby saw the tears of terror and desperation running down his cheeks and heard him howl like a wounded coyote.

Most of them laughed when I hit the snow pile and somersaulted into the bulrushes. I crawled out unhurt, except for my pride.
But then I began to grin. For a minute I had been the centre of attention—something every kid needs now and again.

Pneumonia strikes again

Maybe Mother caught a chill at the skating party anyway she started feeling ill the next day.

Mother had correctly guessed that her old complaint, pneumonia, would return. But she hadn't imagined that the coldest, stormiest two weeks of the winter would arrive with it. After spending three days in bed, getting weaker each day, she realized she had to act.

"Get up Stan," ordered Fred. "Now!"

"School today?" I asked, shaking free the sleepers that hung like icicles from my eyes.

"No school today. The weather's still bad—40 below and blowing snow. Mom is sicker than yesterday," said Fred, sounding grown-up for his years.

I pulled my clothes under the covers and wiggled into them. Racing from the room, I passed the washstand with water frozen solid in the basin and the window layered with frost patterns barring all vision. On the warmer ground floor, Fred placed my breakfast on the table: a bowl of puffed wheat, a slab of bread, and a jug of watery milk from powder.

"The milk is funny," I grumbled.

"You know the cow dried up—it ain't milking now. I mixed milk with water from melted snow, 'cause the well's froze over."

For the last three days, Fred had climbed down into it every day to chop through the ice, but yesterday it had frozen so hard and thick he had given up. I knew all that, but deep inside uncertainty had begun to grow; I reacted by complaining.

"I want oatmeal," I argued.

"Mom's sick! Eat what you got," Fred yelled. "And when you finish, go see Mom—she has a job for you."

Mom had moved a bed into the sitting room so she could easily stoke the Quebec heater. As I entered, she raised her head and spoke: "Stan, I'm too ill to get out of bed. Fred will stay home to look after Joy and me. I want you to go to Schultz's for help."

I thought of the snowdrifts, the terrible cold, the long walk alone and, worst of all, Mr. Schultz's bull. My eyes filled with tears, and I stuttered out the words, "M-mommy . . . they've got . . . a-a bull."

Mom answered, pausing often for breath, "They tie it in the

barn in this weather . . . You need to be brave. A son of Harriet and Fred Stone . . . shouldn't fear anything. We don't have Pop with us so you and Fred . . . must act like grown men."

Mom pushed a note at me: "Take this to Mr. Schultz . . . It asks him to come in his covered rig and . . . take me to town . . . to the hospital. Horses can get through . . . nothing else can. She fell back on the bed gasping for breath.

Wrapped up in double layers of clothing, only my eyes peeking through folds of a heavy scarf, I leaned into the vicious wind. Blowing snow meant I could see only yards ahead. I knew the basic rules: stay on the road allowance between the fences, keep snow from getting on your face or in your boots, and don't stop walking—no matter what, don't stop.

With a half mile still to go, a mountainous snow bank blocked the roadway. The words *stay between the fences*, echoed in my head as I climbed the drift on hands and knees, its wind-hardened crust carrying my weight. Almost over, I stood up, but the crust broke through, dropping me into the snow beneath. For five minute-long seconds, I battled the white grave, broke free and struggled on until I fell against Schultz's back door. I could feel melting snow under my scarf and in my boots.

"It's Harriet's boy, half frozen," cried Mrs. Schultz. While she pulled off my clothes and rubbed snow on the frozen edges of my ears, Mr. Schultz read the note, then headed for the barn.

A half hour later I scraped frost from the little window in Mr. Schultz's van and watched the huge farm horses pulling us through the snowdrifts. Great muscles strained, clouds of frozen breath blasted from nostrils ringed with tiny icicles, and huge feet packed down snow so our sleigh runners could pass. "Ja, ve get your mom soon to the hospital," said Mr. Schultz.

We got Mom to the hospital where she stayed for a week. Mr. Schultz dropped Fred, Joy, and me at various places. I went to the Harris's farm. They lived with their 12 children—my best friend Gord was the youngest—in a low house that looked like a bunch of granaries joined together. I slept in the boys' room, in a lower bunk between Gord and the open studs of an outside wall. I could touch the frosty inner side of the boards that faced the weather.

I really liked Gord. We got along well—in fact we thought of ourselves as relatives because Pop's sister had married Gord's uncle. Gord had red hair and freckles and a florid complexion. About half of his older brothers looked just like him.

For a week I shared the excitement of living as part of a large family: helping Gord with his chores, eating at the huge table, playing Monopoly in the evenings, and listening to voices and sounds of the family settling down to sleep.

With the able help of the Sisters of St. Joseph and the doctor, mother bounced back. We got through that awful winter—one of the worst in years—and into another spring without additional calamities.

To the Lake

The van swayed along with the horses' hooves beating trot-time on the hard earth. With only one week of school remaining, our spirits ran high as spit balls and hard peas propelled from celluloid tubes ricocheted around the cramped interior of the van.

Montana—who had got a new job driving the Roseville van—yelled, "Cut it out! Put them away. Next person who shoots one of those things gets his bottom spanked until it turns bright red."

In the back corner against the door, Rachel Jennings, aged 12, tossed her head sending blond curls bouncing. "And how exactly would you know when a bottom turned red?"

"In your case, I'd look and see," came Montana's response.

Rachel's face turned red while the rest of us, especially the boys, sniggered, but we did put away our pea shooters. I chose to jump into the lull to share some family news Mother had announced only the day before. "We're going to the lake, to Hardisty, for a week this summer."

"Ha, Hardisty isn't a lake; it's just a big slough. Why don't you go to a proper place like Sylvan lake?" said Rachel.

"Because they can't afford to go to a real lake," jeered Ralph, Rachel's little brother.

Fred stepped out of character and spoke up, "We're going there because we like it; we've been before—lots of times."

"Hup, whoa, whoa," Montana called to the team bringing the van bouncing to a stop beside a car halted at the roadside. "Here are your parents."

Ralph pushed past Rachel to jump out first. As Rachel stepped down, she looked back at me and said, "Don't drown in the slough."

I seethed; just because they have an indoor bathroom, a nearly-new Ford, and a big Massey tractor, they think they're . . . they're millionaires. I sure wasn't going to tell them that someone at the church paid the $5.00 for our cabin for the week. But heck, I didn't care; we were going to Hardisty. Then I realized I'd thought the word *heck*; good thing I hadn't said it aloud. If Mother found out she'd skin me alive; to say *heck* was almost as bad as saying *hell.*

School ended, the weeks passed, and we began packing for Hardisty. My excitement grew even more acute when I learned Noel and Aunt Dolly and their daughter Emily had rented a cottage during the same week. Mother began issuing travel orders. "Al Nixon offered to take us. He'll pick us up in the morning. Stan and Joy and I will ride in his back seat because my friend Clara is coming. She can ride in the front with Al. Fred, you'll ride with the preacher who's taking Noel and Aunt Dolly; he'll come by here to pick you up."

Even the thought of riding in a car excited us. "We'll be travelling in twin, blue, four-door 1935 Chevrolets," said Fred. He always knew about such things. He knew about everything.

We loaded into the cars just as mother had said. Before they sped off, Al Nixon called to the other driver, "Beat you there, Reverend."

In 15 minutes, I began to feel sick at the stomach. I always got ill riding in a car and often had to "upswallow."

"Push him over the seat," Clara said. "He might ride better up front."

They accomplished just that without even slowing the car. Mom handed over a chamber pot in case my stomach got seriously upset; Clara seated me between Al and herself and put the chamber pot in her lap. My stomach settled down and I began to enjoy the ride. Sitting up front that way meant I saw it coming.

Speeding along a dirt road, miles ahead of the preacher's car, we started down a slight incline with a farm on the left and a slough on the right. Without any warning, without as much as a honk, a flock of domestic geese marched out of the farmyard onto the road, heading for their morning swim in the slough. Some of them never made it.

Al never even got his foot on the brake—we hit the flock at 40 miles an hour. Feathers exploded over the hood, against the windshield, and disappeared almost instantly into the slipstream. Al never slowed; he barely glanced back at the cloud of feathers settling over the bodies of dead and injured geese. "Ha," he said, "The preacher will come along in 15 minutes and get blamed for that!"

A half hour later, a police car pulled us over just outside Hardisty—they had an RCMP post there. Thoughts of dying geese filled our heads. The policeman strutted toward us, looked the car over carefully, shook his head and approached the driver's window. So the policeman wouldn't see the chamber pot, Clara slipped off her hat, dropping it crown down into the pot with the wide brim covering it completely.

"No problem," the policeman said. "We just had a report of some suspicious people in a blue car. Obviously not you. Have a good trip."

I don't know what did it, maybe the excitement of the trip or the goose collision. Maybe the policeman or the sudden braking when Al stopped for the police car triggered it. In any case, my stomach gave no warning; I turned my head toward the chamber pot and let it go.

Clara didn't react quickly enough; I filled her hat right to the brim.

Hardisty

The cottage had two rooms. A kerosene stove with two burners sat to the right of the door beside a work table. Over the work table hung a rickety cupboard containing dishes and cooking utensils. On the left stood a dining table and six chairs. At the back of the room, a double bed and a sofa flanked the door to the second room. Two double beds and a chest of drawers filled the second room. Oil lamps provided light if we didn't get to bed before dark. Fred and I got the bed in the main room; Mom, Joy, and Clara claimed the back room.

Noel, Aunt Dolly, and Emily had a one-room cottage just a few yards away through the trees.

The lake seemed big to us—two or three times as wide as the big pond in our coulee and much cleaner and deeper. A short pier reached out from a sandy beach. We even had the use of a rowboat, but Mother wouldn't let us go out in it alone. I enjoyed working my way along the side of the pier to a point where my feet just touched the bottom—until a bigger boy put his hand on my head and shoved me under.

Noel rarely came to the beach and Fred paid no attention when I got in trouble. So for the rest of the week, I confined myself to the shallow water and the sand, sailing hand-carved boats and building sand castles. Mom and the rest of the adults had other ideas about what we should do with our vacation time.

The adults wanted to go picking saskatoons—you know, those delicious little blueberries that grow on the prairies. I don't know why they wanted to go berry picking. We had lots of them growing on the farm by the big slough in the south field. But what adults want, they get! The next day just after lunch, carrying an assortment of pails, pots and tin cans, we walked to a bush just off the highway.

All afternoon Fred and I picked berries, got our necks sunburned, slapped mosquitos, and tried to stay out of the adults' range of vision. We would reappear occasionally to dump our few berries into the big buckets to give the impression of busyness. About five o'clock we all marched back to our cottage where Mother and Aunt Dolly began preparing dinner. I remember only one part of the meal: saskatoons covered with rich cream bought from a farmer who delivered to the cottages.

During the evening the ladies dumped the saskatoons into a big pot, covered them with water and started them simmering over the kerosene stove. "We'll walk into town tomorrow, buy a few sealers, and can these," Mother announced.

Just before bedtime, as Noel and Aunt Dolly prepared to take Emily back to their cottage, Mother checked the saskatoons. "Oh, begger!" she said.

The uncharacteristically strong language from Mother brought us all to the stove. She removed the lid allowing all of us to peer in. A scum of small worms covered the surface of the water. Even as we watched, more tiny worms slithered from berries and floated to the top. Noel turned white. Without saying a word, he grabbed a towel, wrapped it around the handles, carried the pot out the door, and dumped berries, worms, and water into the woods.

We all felt our stomachs turn cartwheels, but no one brought up—not even me.

When we got home, Mother canned dozens of saskatoons picked in our own patch. I ate and enjoyed them, but with less enthusiasm than I once displayed.

Old Dick to the rescue

During the winters, Mother would often ride to Gawain in the school van, do her shopping and visiting, and return on the van in the afternoon. Sometimes when she landed a week's work at the hospital or a local business, she would travel back and forth with us in the van every day. Neither the van drivers nor school board seemed to mind. But oh, how she hated depending on others.

"I think I'll buy a car," she announced one day.

"Mom, you can't drive," I said.

Fred jumped in with, "And what about gas rationing?"

"I'll learn to drive. And we'd never go far enough to use much gas—only to town now and again and to Ponoka to see Pop—and to Hardisty once a year."

A few days later a salesman and his helper showed up with two 1920s vintage cars: an Essex or Hudson limousine complete with two little jump seats between the back and front seats, and a dark-blue Dodge sedan. I wanted the limousine; Fred voted for the Dodge. Mother decided against both.

After considering the pros and cons she realized she couldn't afford either. And besides, Fred didn't have the knowledge to look after a car, and she'd likely have a difficult time learning to drive.

So instead Mother bought a buggy with robins-egg blue shafts and a black horse named Captain. She could drive a horse and Fred and I could harness it and look after it. Except she hadn't consulted with Captain—or as we called him, Cap.

Cap shied at every small animal or bird, took the bit between his teeth, made his own decisions, and sometimes chose the ditch rather than share the road with other traffic. It took only one week to realize we had big problems.

"He's too flighty. I can't handle him; he'll kill us," Mom confided to Noel.

"Don't worry," Noel said. I'll take Cap and work off his energy pulling the plow. You can use my horse, Old Dick. He's old and he wouldn't harm anyone."

That's how Old Dick entered our lives. Load three kids on his back and he gladly played cowboys, Indians, and horses; but at one speed only, a slow steady gait all of his own. Hook him to a buggy, and he would cross any prairie, plow through the mud, or follow roads awash with spring runoff. He never even flinched on entering the motorized, down-town traffic of Gawain. On a busy day, that might mean meeting up to 15 cars, farm trucks, and tractors. He simply ignored them and plodded on.

Then came the day that Old Dick permanently etched a place in family folklore.

We set off on the six-mile trip to visit family friends, the Harris's. Six miles at Dick's pace took well over an hour. Mother firmly planted her bulk in the centre of the buggy seat. Joy and I sat one on each side. Summer days in Alberta were special. Dust devils spun away from each plodding step; hawks arced across a clear sky; frogs sang in unison from each roadside slough. Joy and I leaned against mother, forming a human pyramid all three nearly asleep after more than an hour of steady plodding.

None of us, not even Old Dick with his 30 years of horse experience, understood the mechanical intricacies of a kingpin, the device that keeps the front axle, wheels, and shafts attached to the rest of the conveyance. It seems the nut that holds the pin in place slowly worked loose allowing the pin to drop freely to the ground.

We in our summer-induced indolence didn't suspect a thing until our bodies hurtled across the dashboard and landed face down in a neat row on the dirt road. It took a few moments for us to return to reality. Behind us, the front end of the buggy's wooden chassis rested on the road; it sat at 45 degrees with only the rear wheels supporting it. Ahead of us, still in the shafts, plodded Dick—pulling a much lighter load consisting only of front axle and wheels. The reins, only seconds before gripped in Mother's hands, now dangled over the axle and trailed in the dust.

Dick never looked back. His pace remained unchanged. Not once did he question his mission; he had set out to go to the Harris farm, and to the Harris farm he went. If for some reason we didn't wish to stay hitched on behind him, that was our problem, not his.

Mind you, when my buddy Gord Harris looked down the road and saw a horse and what looked like a two-wheeled sulky without a driver heading his way, he came to investigate. He stopped Old Dick outside the Harris's farm gate. The old horse happily returned and waited until Gord and I reassembled the rig.

Discovering my father

I discovered the old magazines before my tenth birthday, just about the time Mother began talking about moving to Ontario. Someone had rolled them up, wrapped them with brown paper, and stored them —along with a cardboard box filled with newspaper clippings—on a shelf in the cellar. I spirited everything to my second-floor room, closed the door, spread the clippings on my bed, and carefully unrolled the magazines. I soon realized I had found a treasure.

Buried in the newspaper clippings, I unearthed a tiny, hard-cover notebook. Small pencilled handwriting filled the pages. I could read almost any printed material, but handwriting often confounded me. As I held the little book, a tingle ran up my arm and through my body. This must be the *Boer War Diary* I had heard Mother mention—the commentary of a scout with the British army in South Africa. I battled again to read it, but gave up after deciphering only four words, "lost another horse today . . ." In my mind I heard the crack of a rifle shot and saw the horse fall as the scout rolled into the protection of the scrub. I put the book away almost reverently; it would have to wait till my reading skills improved.

I turned to the most yellow of the clippings dating to the turn of the century. They told of the wins and records made by a British bicycle racer, dubbed the "Manchester Sizzler" who rode with a club called the Manchester Wheelers. My eyes grew larger as I read of 12-hour endurance tests and cross-country races.

Next I turned to the magazines. They proved to be sports magazines, published in England and dated 1907 to 1909. Some of them contained adventuresome accounts written by a former editor who had emigrated to western Canada. One entitled "On Board a Canadian Liner" recounted his experience travelling to Canada third class, or "steerage" with his wife and four children. On leaving the ship at Halifax, they boarded a "colonist train" bound for Alberta. The account finishes with the family arriving, by farm wagon, at a prairie homestead.

The rest of the clippings, written in the 1920s contained letters to the editor of a Canadian newspaper from an Alberta farmer on a world tour. He had sent reports from Egypt describing the wonder of the pyramids, from India picturing the beauty of the Taj Mahal, from Australia recounting visits with friends, and from Hawaii giving a detailed description of Honolulu. That one ended with an invitation to visit Hawaii and a pun: "Honolulu will honour you-you."

I carefully repacked every item and returned them to the basement shelf. What I read excited me more than any library book. The soldier, cyclist, editor, writer, storyteller, homesteader, and world traveller was in fact one person—Pop, my father!

At first I had a hard time identifying this hero with the aged and often confused man who occasionally visited from the hospital.

I returned to the shoe box again and again, thinking, "One day I'll ride a fast bicycle, go to South Africa and India and Australia and I'll write exciting things too! Just like Pop!"

Section Two: London

Remember your creator
    in the days of your youth,
        before the days of trouble come . . .

Chapter 4

A backward look

Every settler who took up the difficult work of farming the prairie had an earlier existence; none arrived blank or empty; most had previously lived an adventuresome life—otherwise they could never have faced the challenge. Discovering Pop's story in a shoe box helped me appreciate both my parents.

Walking in Pop's shoes

Because I had only a handful of toys and even fewer friends, I developed other means of amusement. When listening to the radio, I could shut my eyes and project the scene on the mirror of my mind. I saw the colour and detail of the clothes worn by the Lone Ranger and Tonto; I felt the rumble of the mighty engine in the Green Hornet's car. I travelled wherever the radio took me.

Rarely did I resist going to bed early. Curling into the fetal position, I would shut my eyes and enter the storybook world of imagination. Every night I rode with the Mounties, tumbled through the skies in a Spitfire, sat at the throttle of a great steam locomotive, or joined an African safari. Often as I slipped into sleep, the fancy followed me into dreamland.

One evening I propped an old picture of Pop against the oil lamp on the orange crate Mother had covered for use as a night table. I slipped into bed, clamped the covers tightly under my chin, and studied the sepia print. A sergeant sat on a duffle bag; on his left another soldier squatted cross-legged on the ground with a third leaning against him. Pop sat to the right of the sergeant, cross-legged, sleeves rolled up, wide-brimmed scout hat on his head. Horses grazed on the African veld beyond the tent. The barrel of a rifle poked from a pile of gear behind the reclining soldier. I shut my eyes, imagining myself as Pop during the Boer War almost a half century earlier. I remembered the entry in his diary: lost another horse today.

When my eyes signalled the approach of the sandman, I blew out the lamp. Sleep quickly overtook me.

In an instant my eyes opened, I rolled from my bedroll, and landed crouching inside the low tent. Before the trumpeter could sound the second note I stood outside on the Transvaal veld. I had slept fully clothed so it took only seconds to pull on boots, pick up my saddle and rifle, and head for the horses. In nearby tents men grumbled and struggled into clothes while I enjoyed the early-morning air and watched a streak of light growing in the northeast.

Always an early riser, I reach full alertness in seconds. My athletic training has built muscles and sharpened reflexes so that few jobs daunt me. The sergeant hadn't known me long when he said, "Private, you're assigned to scout duty." So here I am, preparing to scour the South African veld ahead of the moving battalion, looking for Boer patrols or sharpshooters.

"Steady Bess," I said to my mount as I cinched the saddle. I walked Bess to the cook wagon to rustle up some grub. Too early for breakfast, I settled for a wad of bread and a few rashers of yesterday's salt pork, stuffing extra into my pocket for later. Within minutes of rising I rode through the camp perimeter, called out to the sentries, and headed north-west on the road to Mafeking—if you can call wagon ruts a road.

Thirty minutes out, the veld rose and fell ahead of me in gentle undulations—bare except for scrub African brush and aloes that offered little cover in an attack. A stream crossed the low valley 200 yards from the brow of the next rise. At the drift Bess paused to drink while I studied the ridge ahead. I heard a metallic snick as Bess snapped her head up suddenly. Her body began to sag as the distinctive crack of a Mauser reached my ears. Grabbing my Lee Enfield, I rolled clear of the falling mount. In a continuous motion I came up in a running crouch and dived into thicker bushes at the edge of the stream.

From this safer position I fired three warning shots to signal advance mounted units of the approaching British Army. Looking downstream I could see Bess lying dead by the water's edge. The shooter had spared me by killing Bess with a shot through the heart.

Stretching out in my hiding place I thought about my options: "Fred, stand up or even raise your head and an Afrikaner marksman will pick you off—so wait."

One o'clock arrived with no sign of advancing troops. Maybe enemy activity had convinced them to remain in camp. Whatever the cause, it left me stranded in enemy territory with only my British wit, a Lee-Enfield, little cover, two rashers of salt pork, a chunk of bread, and no horse.

The scrub brush offered no cover from the sun above. Without showing myself, I wiggled closer to the stream, filled my hat with water, and eased slowly back. Two Widow birds rose to my left, almost belatedly, their long tails pointing toward me as though signalling the enemy.

I heard the hiss and ricochet of the bullet a second or so ahead of the rifle's report. It struck a few yards down stream near where the birds had appeared. They don't know my exact position! My mind raced over the facts: about a second's delay between the strike and report; the sound came from the north-east; only one shot. So it came from the same ridge as the shot that killed Bess—that likely means only one man pinning me down.

The water had drained from my hat, so I repeated the procedure. No shot disturbed me as I drank my fill and topped up my canteen. Peering through the leaves, I could see the ridge. Even as I watched, a black slouch hat appeared, then vanished. "Aha," I thought, "One man, and just as afraid to show himself as I am."

Thinking the head might reappear, I reached for my rifle, gripping the exposed metal barrel. The Boer on the hill must have heard my cry as I snatched back my burned hand. Will I ever get used to the heating power of the African sun? I slid forward and dunked my hand in the stream. "Dumb idea," I chastised myself, "I could never hit him at this range. But he easily out-guns me and wouldn't miss. I'll wait till dark to make my move."

As darkness closed in, I dozed, but became fully alert at the sound of movement on dried grass. In the dim light I saw hundreds of shadows on both sides of the stream: gemsbok; springbok or impala; and huge elands. At first I stared at them, thinking they could feed the whole battalion for a month. Then the idea struck: with my right hand, I pawed in the stream for throwing stones, gripped my Lee-Enfield in my left, leaped to my feet, and ran at the herd like a madman, yelling and throwing stones.

The animals ran in all directions, filling the night with a cloud of confusion and dust. I started southeast in a running, zig-zagging crouch. After three hours of stiff walking I mounted a low koppie and spotted the encampment—for whatever reason they had not moved on. I broke into a mile-eating lope and arrived at the perimeter 30 minutes later.

"Rat-a-tat-tat," a machine gun greeted me, ripping up dirt on both sides of the trail.

"Dorchester! Dorchester!" I screamed the password and waved my hat.

When I awoke the next morning, the sepia picture had tumbled from the orange crate to the floor.

I hurried downstairs to tell Mom about my weird dream. As I finished it with a flurry of dramatics, dancing to demonstrate how Pop avoided the machine gun fire from his own side, I saw something I had never seen before. A tear rolled from under Mom's glasses and down her cheek.

"Your father was, is, a very brave man. He won a medal for bravery, for doing something few men would ever do. One time while on scout duty he became separated from his unit. Late in the day he found an injured Boer soldier lying on the ground, unconscious."

"Just exactly what are Boers?" I butted in. I figured that since I'd dreamt about them, I should know what they are.

"Dutch farmers whose people had settled South Africa years ago. The British and the Boers got into a war for control of South Africa. Anyway, Pop bound up the enemy soldier's wounds, put him on his own horse and began leading it toward the British position. As night fell, he realized he could get back only by passing through enemy lines."

I furrowed my forehead over the words "enemy lines," but didn't interrupt again.

"So Pop muffled the horse's feet with pieces of clothing and sneaked through the Boer camp. He got back safely to his own lines and delivered his wounded enemy to the field hospital. The Queen of England pinned a medal on him for that brave action."

Mom wiped another tear from her cheek and turned to the cupboard to begin preparing lunch. I stared at her broad back, wondering why having a hero for a husband would make her shed tears.

Mother also went to war

Mother told stories better than anyone I knew. She could "spin a yarn" as Grandpa Johanson used to say, but she also had packed a lot of adventure into her life. Unlike Pop, who seemed reluctant to talk about his war, Mother delighted in sharing hers. She had joined the Women's Army Auxiliary Corp, or WAACs, of the British army as a cook at the beginning of the Great War. When they shipped her off to France, things got exciting.

When times got a little dull around our house, we'd plead, "Mother, tell us about the war. Tell us about France."

And Mother would begin to talk. One day she asked, "Did I ever tell you about the day I got drunk on a nickel?"

Even though we'd heard the story at least a dozen times, Fred and I dutifully showed astonishment—Mother never drank. She laughed and began her story. "We were in France. Stationed just outside Bologne. My friend Ruth and I went for a walk on a hot day. Wore our uniforms, of course. Wouldn't dare leave camp without them—the British government wanted its WAACs to make the best impression. We didn't usually go far—wanted to stay near the camp in case the Jerry's air-bombers came over and we needed the air-raid shelters."

"So did they come that day?" Fred asked.

"Nope. But it was such a lovely day we walked further than usual. The more we walked, the hotter we got. We found a small park with trees and stopped for rest. Met a few old folks and a few mothers with children there. Had fun trying out our bad French—got a few good laughs. Then a young man came and greeted us in bad English.

"We exchanged pleasantries, and I asked where we could get a cold drink—lemonade or something. He told us about a good bistro further up the road. Even offered to take us there. We told him 'no thanks; we can find it.' Because the bistro was on the way to the camp, we thought it a convenient place to stop."

At this point Mother remembered she had bread in the oven and hurried to the kitchen to check it. We followed her there. Even while lifting the loaves from the oven, she continued the story. "We found the bistro, a dark, dingy place, and went in. The seedy crowd quit talking and stared at us as we stepped up to the bar. 'Lemonade please,' Ruth ordered in English. The bartender nodded, said something in French, and went out back. He brought out two tall glasses of lemonade."

"I'll bet it was booze," Fred suggested. I wondered where he'd heard that big word.

Mother shook her head. "It looked and tasted like lemonade. I tipped it up and swallowed half a glass. Ruth tasted hers, spit it back, and grabbed me by the arm, spilling my drink on the counter. She dragged me outside and started us running for the camp. Couldn't figure out what was wrong with her, because I started feeling pretty good. When we reached the camp, I had my hat in one hand, my coat in the other, and was singing at the top of my voice. I'd have been in real trouble if an officer had seen me."

Mother selected a tiny loaf made from a small piece of left-over dough, broke it in two, and gave a half to each of us.

"What was wrong with your drink?" I asked as I bit into the treat.

"Knock-out drops. The authorities later closed the place. They'd drug soldiers, rob them, and then throw them in the back alley. Heaven knows what might have happened if Ruth hadn't caught on. Times haven't changed that much—we had some real rotters back then too."

One day when our mutual buddy Bert had dropped in for a visit with Fred and me, it began raining, sending us indoors.

"Mom, tell Bert about when you were in the army," Fred said.

"You were a lady soldier? Did you carry a gun?" Bert shot back incredulously.

Mother laughed as she answered, “Oh no. We went to war as cooks, nurses, and clerks. They didn’t give us guns; we fought the war with cooking pots, bed pans, and notebooks.”

“Was it fun?” Bert asked.

“Fun? War is never fun. It’s pain and death and horror. It’s fear and sickness . . .,” Mother paused for a long moment, stared at Bert, and then went on. “Yes, and it is fun when you’re young and away from home for the first time.”

Thinking Mom might get too serious, I cut in, “Mom, tell us about the air-bombers and the air-raid skelters.”

Mother always called enemy planes air-bombers.

“You mean, air-raid shelters,” my know-it-all brother volunteered.

Mother began her story. “When the sirens sounded we ran for cover in underground rooms called, as Fred said, air-raid shelters. Each air-bomber carried two bombs on a teeter-totter thing. The airman pushed one bomb off and the other fell a few seconds later. One evening we girls had just made it into the shelter when a bomb fell near the camp. Most of us froze in terror, knowing the next might land closer, could kill us all. But nothing scared Ruth. She sat on a ledge half-way up the wall, laughing, and taunting, ‘Jerries can’t hit nothin’, Jerries can’t hit nobody.'

“Just then the second bomb exploded outside, blasting us all against the far wall. I saw Ruth flying end-over-teakettle into the middle of the room and landing on the dirt floor. She got up, shook herself and said, ‘I don’t mind Jerry dropping his bombs. But I wish he wouldn’t throw dirt in my face.’ The rest of us forgot our fear and roared with laughter.”

Bert asked, “Why did they attack a camp full of women?”

“Didn’t know we were women, I guess. Our boys, the British army, had placed guns on nearby hills to shoot at the air-bombers. One day as they attacked the city, the soldiers at one gun loaded and fired as fast as they could into the air above our camp. The shells exploded above us like fireworks as we ran for the shelter. We later heard that a senior officer rushed up to the gun crew and yelled, ‘Don’t fire that way; the bombers are over the city. There are no planes where you're firing.' The captain in charge of the gun roared back, 'No there aren't, and there aren't going to be; that's where the girls are!'"

The end of Mother's war

One chilly November day I rolled out two large sheets of brown paper and began to draw pictures—war pictures. In the early '40s, the radio and the newspapers never missed a chance to make real to all of us the war raging in Europe. Every child played war games and dreamed of growing up to join the air force, navy, or army—usually in that order. As I played, an awful thought began troubling me: what if the war ended before I got old enough to go? What if I missed it?

I abandoned my play and raced downstairs. "Mom, what if the war ends before I get to go?"

Mother's mouth pinched into a straight line, her forehead wrinkled, and her brown eyes turned almost black. The change frightened me. She seated me on a kitchen chair, and said in a harsh voice, "You don't want to go to war, believe me."

She sat for a long moment before relaxing and becoming my old mother again. Then she told a story with such vivid reality that I can close my eyes today and retell it to you as if I had watched the scene unfold.

Mother stood ram-rod straight at the edge of a great open grave; bodies wrapped in blankets formed neat rows just below her. Near silence, broken only by the distant chirp of birds, pressed in on her. A grey overcast sky echoed back a sense of oppression.

The sudden intrusion of a bugle caused her to shut her eyes and pull a psychological blanket over her head and heart. Only years of strict parade-ground training stopped trembling hands from covering fearful ears. Her legs became rubber—her body swayed.

These boys, wrapped and aligned with military precision, heard neither birds nor bugle or saw the leaden sky. They knew nothing of the young women in khaki uniforms nor their battle-worn comrades formed up behind. They did not feel the press of foreign soil at their backs or anticipate a permanent, comfortless, earthen cover.

These boys, laughing and cheering in a show of bravado, had gone up the line just days before. They had passed through the cook camp, queued up at the kitchen, filled their mess kits, then retreated to the trees or parade square to eat a last meal before the great battle. Most had joked and flirted with the girls and hoped to meet them again on their return. They even dreamed of taking one of them back home—after they got the job done.

Her legs buckled and her body began to arc forward toward those who had paid the sacrifice, toward death, toward eternity. But strong arms from either side and behind caught her at the brink and pulled her back into the land of the living.

She told me that story in November one year. Even then as she spoke of the horrors of her war, another raged across the same lands in Europe. I went to my room and sat beside a miniature airport, drawn on brown wrapping paper. I picked up a toy Spitfire and stared out the window into another leaden sky. War had lost its appeal. I had heard other war stories—tales of adventure, fun, and comradeship—but death had now added a new dimension. The scene at the mass grave had put a stranglehold on a seed growing in my young life.

Although I still dreamed of hurtling through the heavens in a machine of war, a feeling of uncertainty came with it.

Mother told us many other war stories. She also told how the continual bombing had broken her health so that the medical corp returned her to England suffering shell shock.

Following recovery and demobilization, Mother gladly said goodbye to England and immigrated to peaceful, pastoral Canada in order to flee the memories of war-ravaged Europe. She settled in London, Ontario.

Mother's other life

Not all Mother's wonderful stories came out of the war.

Again and again she told us about her courtship and marriage to Pop. After losing his second wife, Pop remembered meeting Mother. She had visited the farm a year or two earlier when travelling west from Ontario on vacation with a friend. They had come to the farm so the friend could visit her Uncle Fred—Pop of course. So Pop courted Mom by mail.

Mom travelled west to marry him early in 1931.

One day Fred and I sat at the kitchen table eating pancakes with corn syrup. Mother had put the syrup in a little brown jug; we usually poured it right from the tin.

"During that first summer on the farm," she said, "I stood here at the kitchen window with my hands on my hips looking out at a glorious day waiting for Pop to return from town. I was happy because I knew we would have a baby—you Fred. I remember singing a hymn."

That seemed pretty ordinary to me; Mother always stood with her hands on her hips and she sang most of the time. In fact that big voice of hers could rattle the glass in the kitchen windows. I did wonder why expecting to give birth to Fred would make anyone happy.

Mother dropped another pancake on my plate and continued, "I heard a loud humming sound and stopped singing. The hum became a roar, then the sky darkened as a terrible dust storm struck. I saw boards, litter, and one poor chicken tumbling across the yard. Then it turned as black as midnight."

"Gosh," said Fred, "just like it did last month."

Mother nodded. "Much worse. And don't say gosh, it's just a substitute for using God's name. Yes, much worse. Terrified me. Imagined myself back in France and began to go into shock. In the roar of the wind I heard approaching air-bombers; the blackness of the room took me back to the darkness of an air-raid shelter.

"Then I had what I thought at first was a wonderful vision—like a knight approaching on a white horse. In fact a white horse did gallop past the window. Pop came rushing in and lit an oil lamp. He'd heard the storm coming and galloped the horses all the way. Drove them and the democrat right into the shed. He knew the dust storm would terrify me.

"Later when the storm cleared, Pop went out to care for the team and collect the things he had bought. When he came back indoors, he handed me a brown-paper bag. My hands were shaking so hard from the fear of the storm, I could hardly open it. Pop had bought me a present. First thing he ever got me."

Mother lifted the little brown jug from the table. "I found this in the bag with a jar of imitation maple syrup. Pop said something about it being a symbol of Canada, even though we don't have maple trees in Alberta. Then he asked me if I wanted to move back to Ontario—or better yet, after the baby comes, back to England. Pop said he always had dreamed of buying a little corner of old England."

I poured some more corn syrup from the little jug onto my pancake and asked, "What does a maple tree look like?"

Chapter 5

Ontario beckons

The storms get worse

About five years had passed since the heavy hand of tragedy had struck down Pop, inflicting him with mental illness and taking him from us.

On a summer afternoon, we stood together at the kitchen window. The sky had turned an eerie colour and a powerful wind drove litter across the yard and battered the old farm. It moved the great machine shed from its foundations and began shaking a wooden gate the way a cat shakes a mouse. The gate, made of four ten-foot-by-ten-inch boards mounted in a metal frame, joined the farm yard to the lane that dipped into the gully.

Mother, expecting the house to go, prepared to rush us to the basement at the first sign of disaster. As we watched, the wind ripped the gate's heavy boards one at a time. First the top board snapped, then the next, until all splintered and the wind tossed the halves of the gate aside like a torn sheet of paper. We stood there for what seemed like hours until the storm abated during the evening.

The next day, we walked around the farm surveying the damage; the two halves of the gate, reduced to kindling and bent iron; the machine shed sitting askew, four feet off the foundation at one end; boards and shingles torn from the barn and chicken house; and litter trapped along the fences.

The next week the authorities at Ponoka sent Pop home again, saying, "Feed him well and don't let him worry."

During one lucid week Pop arranged for neighbours to put the machine shed back on its foundation and dig in three "dead-man" anchors so it wouldn't move again. By the second week he began to lose touch. During the third week Al Nixon came to calm him and help him into the back seat of a police cruiser.

Mother teetered on the very edge herself as symptoms of shell shock began to return. She visited Dr. Rich to appeal for medication, but what he prescribed didn't come out of a bottle. "Harriet," he said, "Get out. Take the kids and go back east to your sister. If you stay here, they'll keep sending your husband home until you break and end up in the mental hospital with him."

When she returned home, we stood at the kitchen window looking toward the barn where simple wire strands replaced the wooden and iron gate. Mother had made a decision. "I'm not a quitter," she said, "and this has been the hardest decision of my life. But if we don't get out of here, this God-forsaken country will break each one of us the way the wind broke the gate."

A year or two before Mother made her momentous decision, local township officials had intervened on our behalf and instigated a 'mother's allowance' payment of $30 per month. She never could understand why government would take with one hand and then give back with another. She mused, "Had we stayed in England, the lot of us would have ended up in a poor house—this is better, but I still don't like being on welfare."

The harsh weather, poverty, government duplicity, emotional stress, and the doctor's advice pushed Mother to the only possible decision. Within days she had written Aunt Elsie and posted hand-written flyers advertising our things for sale. She set a date for the sale that would give her time to prepare.

We'd soon move to London, Ontario! Mother would find a job; we'd attend a big school; and no more howling dust storms or school vans!

An RCMP raid

Before the sale day arrived, a mountie came to our door—the RCMP police the province of Alberta. The mountie, a young man who looked embarrassed at confronting a woman, waved a sheaf of papers at Mother. "The public administrator sent me to inform you that you cannot sell and move away. You cannot sell anything on this property that belongs to your husband."

Mother stiffened. "I don't plan to sell anything that belongs to my husband."

"Your notice of sale listed a separator. That would be the grain separator, the threshing machine in the shed out back. That belongs to your husband," insisted the officer.

"Come in," Mother ordered. "I see someone fed bad information to the public administrator. Or did you come to that wrong-headed conclusion all by yourself?"

The mountie removed his hat and followed Mom to the kitchen while Fred and I, in awe, peeked in from the next room. "Do you see that?" asked Mom. "That's a cream separator. I listed that for sale. You pour milk in the top and get cream and skim milk from the spouts while one of the boys turns the handle. I bought it and the cow that provides the milk from money earned cutting vegetables for the hospital kitchen."

"Yes ma'am, I know what a cream separator is. I guess we have wrong information."

Mom then marched the officer into the living room and showed him the couch she had bought with money made plucking turkeys for the local butcher. She led him around the house pointing to other items she planned to sell and explained how she had bought them with her own money. Then she demanded, "Now you tell me, do these things belong to me or to my husband?"

The officer said, "They're yours ma'am."

Then he stood at attention by the door, put on his wide hat, and said, "Ma'am, I must do my duty. The public administrator sent me to inform you that you cannot sell these things and leave."

Next he removed his hat, placed it over his heart, smiled, and said, "I just spoke officially as a policeman. Now I'll speak as a man. Go ahead—sell your things and move. They can't touch you."

Then he bowed to Mother, winked at Fred and me, and walked out the door.

Tippy checks out

"Two weeks," Mother said, waving the train tickets as she stepped down from the buggy. "Two weeks from today, we leave for Ontario."

My brother hurried to unhitch Old Dick. He'd leave the buggy near the house and walk the horse to the barn to unharness him. I helped my little sister climb down from her high perch on the seat and then collected the small box of groceries from the back. Even in little things like this, we each had our assigned tasks—well, most of us had our appointed tasks. The moment Joy's feet touched the ground, she ran after Mother. I guess you shouldn't expect too much from a five-year-old.

Tippy raced around me in tight circles, yapping continuously as though the box contained a treat. Which it didn't—Tippy got nothing but scraps of human food. If they had invented dog food back then, we certainly couldn't afford it. Everybody, except Joy and me, considered Tippy a useless cur. He and Joy loved each other; I looked on him as a close friend.

I placed the box on the old work table we'd brought in from the lean-to. Mother's sale had gone well; she had sold the kitchen furniture and almost everything else in the house. "Anything else need doing, Mom?" I asked.

"No, thank you. Go out and play with Tippy while you can," she answered.

I'd made it to the coulee bank with Tippy yapping at my heels, when I realized what she said. It hadn't occurred to me that Tippy might not go with us!

I sat cross-legged on the brow of the bank looking at three ponds below framed in green bulrushes. On the almost windless day, the still ponds reflected the brilliant blue of the prairie sky. Three hawks soared in great circles overhead, ready to pounce on unsuspecting creatures below. Tippy, as though suspecting danger from above or some other unknown source, pushed under my arm from behind and licked my face. What would happen to Tippy?

Maybe my friend Gord would take him. Or maybe Noel and Dolly would look after him, or one of the other neighbours—except they all considered him useless. I hugged him, rose to my feet, and returned to the house.

Inside, I sat on an apple crate cum chair. "Mom, can't Tippy go with us?"

"No," she answered, turning away from me. "He's a country

dog. He couldn't live in the city. A day or two before we leave, Mr. Schultz is coming to get . . . to . . . to shoot him."

A horrible chill ran down my back; I couldn't speak. Anyway, you couldn't argue with Mother. I raced from the house, through the garden, and across the summer fallow, finally stopping at the old straw pile by the slough. I threw myself face down and began shaking with great sobs.

After a few minutes I knew what I'd do. I'd go back for Tippy and we'd both run away. When I rolled over and sat up, I found myself looking straight into Tippy's big brown eyes. He licked my face, then spun around and began running toward the house, glancing back to make sure I'd follow.

I broke into a run, laughing, crying, and muttering, "Oh, Tippy, they're right. You're useless. You don't even know enough to run away."

We say goodbye

I gripped a plywood sheet, trying to hold it steady at the bottom while Fred, standing on a rickety ladder, nailed the top to the upper frame of the kitchen window. A burst of north wind sent a shiver up the sheet.

"Hold the damn thing still," Fred yelled.

"You watch your language. Boy, if Mother heard you, she'd leave you here 'stead of taking you to Ontario."

Fred angrily banged home four nails, came down the ladder to fasten the bottom, and said, "Staying here'd suit me just fine."

"Well, we're all going," I grumbled back, grabbing the ladder and starting for the front of the house.

Fred followed, carrying an armful of boards. "Don't you want to go either?"

"I . . . I think so. It's just that we're leaving everything—the house, the farm, the coulee, and Pop. When'll we see Pop again? And . . . I'll miss Tippy."

Fred began nailing boards over the dining room window, starting at the bottom and working upward. About half way up he looked down and said, "I'll come back when I grow up. Maybe we all will. Everything will still be here except for Tippy. He's under the ground."

I wiped my eyes with my sleeve.

"Don't start blubbering. Aunt Dolly was right when she said your bladder's too close to your eyes. Get me some more nails."

We worked our way around the house, sometimes in silence, sometimes arguing. While I carried the few leftover boards to the machine shed, Fred locked the back door with the big iron key and put it in his pocket. "Let's go," he said.

We headed toward the road, carrying the few tools we'd borrowed from Susan and Eric who had moved in with Grandma following Grandpa's death. We'd stay at their place tonight and leave early in the morning. Eric, driving Grandpa's old brown Chev, had picked up our old steamer trunk and some boxes earlier in the day. He'd taken them to the station in Gawain, then returned for Mom and Joy and the carry-on stuff, taking them home with him. Just before Fred had started nailing up the windows, various neighbours had dropped by to pick up the remaining furniture.

I glanced back at the house as we started down the gully toward the road. It stood there—silent, alone, empty, and boarded up. Again I wiped my eyes with my sleeve, but Fred didn't notice.

That night, following a late supper, Grandma Johanson arranged our sleeping. With no beds to spare, she made room for Fred and me in the living room. For a mattress she placed two cow hides on the floor and covered them with sheets and quilts. "Grandpa got these when he ran a butcher business," she explained.

Despite the hard bed, Fred fell asleep immediately. I remained awake listening to the noises of the night slipping in through an open window. Not that prairie nights have much sound, but stillness on the plains has its own presence—like the hum of a hundred distant heartbeats or the faint, eerie song of the northern lights.

Then far away, a coyote howled. Its initial "yip-yip" turned into a cry that rose in pitch and volume and then faded away. I imagined him exploring our empty farmyard in a vain search for chickens. Picturing him sniffing over Tippy's grave, I dragged my sleeve across my eyes. "No coyotes in the city," I thought. "But then no

Tippy either."

The next morning passed in a whirl. We got up and dressed, rolled up the cow hides, ate breakfast, and loaded the car. We had to catch the Edmonton train in Gawain by eight o'clock. Susan rode up front with Eric. The four of us piled into the back seat with our feet on our suitcases. What he couldn't get inside, Eric had tied to the back luggage rack.

Joy sat on Mom's lap. As we passed our place, Mom fussed with Joy's hair, never once looking out the window. I did look, but wished I hadn't. The rising sun lit up the house's upper windows while the lower seemed blindfolded or gagged. I wanted to cry, but I didn't. As the car breasted the hill, Eric slipped it into top gear and sped at 25 miles an hour along the dusty, dirt road. We really had started for Ontario.

I heard Mom speaking to Susan. "We will come back. I'll have to come back every year to visit Pop at Ponoka."

All aboard!

We steamed out of Gawain to the waves and best wishes of Susan, Eric, and three neighbours. A belching, black steam locomotive with tender, a mail and baggage car, an old wooden passenger coach, four box cars, and a caboose, made up the train. With only six other passengers aboard the coach, we easily found seats. "It's a milk run," Mother said. "It stops at every pillar and post along the way."

It took nearly all day to reach Edmonton, where we changed to what mother called a "transcontinental." From the platform we could see neither the engine nor the rear of the train. We climbed aboard and with the help of a conductor found seats half way along a day coach. Fred immediately flipped the back of one seat, so instead of having two bench seats facing forward, we now had two seats facing each other—on our first day out he had become a seasoned traveller.

Fred and I arranged our bags and boxes on the luggage rack. Mom placed the metal food hamper on the seat between herself and Joy. She had enough food jammed into the hamper and a cardboard box to last three days. At meal times, tea pot in hand, she'd head to the kitchen next to the dining car to get boiling water. With that important task done, she would make sandwiches for all of us.

Indeed, as the train raced eastward across the prairies, the trip became an ongoing picnic. We crowded closely around Mother at meal times as she delved into the hamper and pulled out food items: bread, carved ham, tomatoes, cucumbers, carrot sticks, cookies, apples, and raisins. People across the aisle watched us with interest and looked for occasions to talk to us.

"Excuse me ma'am," said a gentleman leaning across the aisle, "Do you have the time? My watch has stopped."

"Mmmm," Mother answered, unable to speak because she had just sunk her teeth into a sandwich.

Still chewing her food, she rooted into the hamper, all the while nodding to assure the man she had understood the question. From deep in the hamper she withdrew an alarm clock and aimed the face toward him. A chuckle ran through the people seated nearby.

Between meals we watched the passing countryside. At first we saw farmers working dusty fields with varied farm implements towed by horses or ancient tractors. Later in the day our windows looked out on abandoned farms: houses with broken windows and sagging doors; farm machines, even old cars and tractors, grown over with weeds; and fields that looked like scenes in a picture book of an arid African desert.

We hurtled through villages, some as desolate as the worst farms, others full of life and people. We stopped only in the larger towns, sometimes long enough for passengers to get out and walk the platforms or even dash to shops. Mother, afraid she might lose us, made us remain in our seats, even when the train man said, "We'll be here for 20 minutes taking on water and coal."

Our spirits always rose when the engine sounded its whistle and the starting jolt rattled through the coach and down the train. Soon we'd get back to full speed, the rails singing their travelling song to the steady chucka-chucka of steel wheels on steel track.

Fred, his face pressed against the window, pocket watch in his hand, looked for the white mileage markers on the telegraph poles.

"Wow, 60! we're going 60 miles an hour."

"How do you know?" I challenged.

"Because it takes us exactly one minute to get from one mile marker to the next—that's a mile a minute or 60 miles an hour."

I may have said it before, but Fred knew everything. I shrugged and headed for the toilet at the end of the coach. I stopped for a drink at the water fountain beside the toilet door. I didn't need a drink; I wanted to see, no I wanted to experience, the tiny paper cups—paper that actually held water!

Having grown up with water in buckets and outdoor toilets, all indoor plumbing fascinated me. Before sitting down, I stared into the porcelain toilet bowl and watched the ties racing by below. As I sat and did my business, I wondered what happened when it struck the ties at 60 miles per hour. My captivation with railway toilets likely accounted for my lack of constipation during the trip.

When bedtime arrived, Fred and I found empty bench seats and curled up under blankets pulled from one of Mother's boxes. Mother propped up her feet on the opposite seat and slept sitting up with Joy snuggled against her.

We awoke before sunrise and watched the black sky turn pink, then red. Finally, a great yellow orb rose from the prairie ahead of us. It seemed as though our train rushed for it as a dart seeks the bull's eye.

To me, the most thrilling times came when the prairies gave way to a wilderness of trees, rocks, and lakes.

I had become much more adventuresome and began exploring the train. In the process I discovered the platforms between the cars where the train men could open doors to allow passengers off or on the train. The sections of the steel floor joining the cars vibrated, adding to the overall excitement. Sometimes, I would find the upper half of the door to the outside fastened open.

Finding the top section of a door open, I stuck my head into the slipstream of cool air infused with smoke and ashes from the engine. Despite the rush of wind on my face, I clearly heard the sound thundering from the giant, Canadian National, four-eight-four, steam locomotive as it rushed across Northern Ontario. The higher-pitched chucka-chucka sound of wheels on track blended with the steady, even beat from the engine's great cylinders.

I looked out on rocks, lakes, and trees flashing by at mile-a-minute speeds. Pushing my head out into the cutting wind and supporting myself with my arms on the top of the half door, toes just touching the floor, I looked forward about half the train's length to see the engine leaning into a banked curve. Black smoke belched from its stack and, trapped by the slipstream, threw itself against the coaches. It stung my eyes and scraped at my throat, but I fearlessly held to my exhilarating position.

The rhythm picked up very slightly. I squinted against the smoke and cinders and imagined myself in the cab of the locomotive watching the actions that brought the change. In my mind I saw the engineer pulling a gold watch from an overall pocket. He first checked the time, looked at the green signal lights along the track, then opened the throttle a little further. Getting the message, the fireman checked the pressure gauge and leapt into action. He gazed into the roaring inferno of the firebox before making adjustments to the auger bringing the black fuel from the coal tender. He next manipulated other controls to increase air flow to the hungry fire.

Slowly the metallic, hammering beat picked up and the blast of air on my face increased. My left hand gripped my brother's pocket watch—he'd kill me if he knew I had it—especially with it protruding out of the train. It had a tiny second hand set into the lower part of the face. I looked for the next white mileage marker, my eyes blinking against the soot and smoke. When the marker flashed by I watched the progress of the tiny hand. At 55 seconds the next marker appeared. "Wow," I yelled into the wind, "Way over 60 miles an hour!"

Beneath my toes the metal floor plates picked up the rhythm and sent it through my whole body. I could feel my hands and arms pulsating, and my legs trembling in time with the throbbing power. Never in all of my ten years had I moved so fast or experienced anything like this!

My ecstatic moment ended as a train man appeared, "Sorry, lad. You can't stand there at this speed. The top half of that door should be closed."

I reluctantly eased back. As he slammed the door and pulled the latch, trees, lakes, rocks, and excitement vanished.

The cops come for Fred

In three and a half days, we arrived in London, Ontario, and moved in with Aunt Elsie, Uncle Sam, and their four boys. As a naive just-turned ten country boy, I had a lot to learn. I had never seen a tree I couldn't wrap my arms around. I hadn't ridden on a bus since England, had never seen a boy scout, rarely walked on a cement sidewalk, or heard more than one airplane in the sky at one time.

For the first few weeks in London I spent a lot of time staring upward—upward at the great maple trees that arched over the streets. Mom had told us about maples and maple syrup; now I could see them. Where the tree canopy opened to the sky, I continued staring—now at the airplanes. I recognized Harvards, Ansons, and Mosquito bombers I had previously seen only in pictures.

Our youngest cousin, Frank, two years older than Fred, introduced Fred to the neighbourhood boys. Just a week later, the police arrived at the door looking for Frank and Fred. A witness had identified them as participants in a raid on a neighbour's garden.

"Two weeks," Mother roared, "and the police come looking for you! Nothing like this ever happened out west. Maybe we should move back."

Following that incident, Mom got tougher, gathering her three kids about her like a mother hen—maybe more like a female bear. She warned us about associating with bad company. She did not want the police looking for one of her boys again.

Within a month she bought an old house complete with furniture for $100 down and $12 per month. We moved to our new home on Wellington Road, a house with antique furniture, outdated wiring, peeling wallpaper, and cracked plaster. But it had heat in every room—in this house the furnace worked! "We'll be healthier and have a great Christmas this year," Mother said.

Now on our own in the big city, Mother enlarged the scope of her admonitions. She warned about traffic, telling us never to play on the busy street in front of our house, not even on the verge between sidewalk and roadway. Soon after, a car swerved onto the sidewalk a half block from our house and crushed two children to death. That increased our respect for Mother's wisdom.

She warned us about strangers and "perverts" who would "interfere" with us if they got the chance. Life changed as we began adjusting to the big city.

At night, lying in my bed, I could hear the whistle of steam locomotives—great black monsters pulling their trains from London to other parts of Canada. Some would find their way to Alberta; maybe I should climb aboard one and head back to my friends Gord and Bert, to the old farm, and to the coulee.

Latch-key kids

Mom had taken a job in the kitchen at Victoria hospital. That meant she left for work before Fred and I headed out for school; she returned an hour after we came home. Mother made me carry the big, old-fashioned key on a cord about my neck. Fortunately, we didn't have to worry about Joy; Aunt Elsie and Uncle Sam had volunteered to keep her for a year. Their daughter had died a dozen years earlier in a diphtheria epidemic.

For the most part, I revelled in city life, but I did have some bad moments. Although I didn't feel any fear of strangers, I found something much more immediate to provoke apprehension. For the first few months in our home next to the dry cleaners, I lived in terror of Old Alligator Mouth.

To guard their premises, the dry cleaners kept a huge German Shepherd tied to an iron post in the back yard. He had tiny evil eyes, an alligator-sized mouth, and salivated whenever I went near his property. Although no one else believed me, I knew he would attack and kill if the opportunity came along. I also knew he would do it one piece at a time, first tearing off my arms and legs, then ripping off my head to finish the job.

Occasionally, this monster would break his chain and patrol the street in front of his property. He did that only at night or early morning. I knew it happened because they had forgotten to feed him and he had broken free to search out some little kid to eat. I didn't care in the evenings when I could stay in the house. I didn't worry as long as mother remained home. As a WAAC in the Great War, she had learned to take care of herself. When she went into her sergeant-major act, everyone, man, woman, or beast, backed off.

One morning, with Mother gone an hour before school time, and Fred away a few minutes ahead of me, I saw the monster parading up and down the street. I knew I'd had it. If I skipped school, the teacher might understand, but she would tell Mother. I began to think I would rather face the monster than the sergeant major.

I screwed up my courage and waited for my chance. When Old Alligator Mouth reached the far end of his beat, I raced across the street and into the alley. The board fences that lined each side offered good protection. When the dog reached the open end of the alley, I ducked into a backyard and waited for him to disappear before racing further along the alley.

I made it to school, late, soaked with perspiration, and shaking with fear. On that day, I really did want to go back to the farm.

Chapter 6

Becoming community

Recognized

We didn't often ride the bus; it cost money, about 12 trips for a dollar. Fred and I walked to school, Mother walked to work, and on Sunday we hoofed it together to church. Going to either of the churches Mother had attended when she had first arrived in Canada would have meant bus travel, so we went to a small church not far from home. We knew no one there.

I think Mother felt a little guilty about our lack of church attendance in Gawain—a want of transportation had stopped us in the early days of Pop's illness, although sometimes the pastor had sent a car to pick us up for special meetings. By the time we got Old Dick, I guess we had got out of the habit. Mom decided to change things when we arrived in Ontario.

We always sat together in church. I sat on one side of Mother, Joy on the other, with Fred at the aisle end of the pew. On the fourth Sunday, during congregational singing, Mother finally felt at home and pulled out all the stops. Her great voice soared above the others and reverberated off the walls. She filled the building with the power and quality of an opera diva. The volume of the singing faded slightly as people wavered between participating and listening to Mother. Across the aisle two women—one tall and skinny, one short and fat—stared at Mother, then began an animated but whispered conversation.

I knew Mother could sing, but I had never seen people react like this. A sense of unease came over me. Pride made me want to stand straight and tall, but embarrassment at having so many people staring impelled me to duck behind Mom's ample frame.

After the service when the two ladies approached us, we learned the content of their whispered conversation. It went like this.

"Isn't that Harriet? She used to sing in London churches 15 years ago."

"It can't be. I heard she went west, got married, then moved to England."

"Well if it is her, she's back with three kids."

Of course they had it right; the Harriet they knew had indeed returned. The chance visit to our little church by the two women had a positive outcome.

The same two ladies appeared at our door one afternoon asking for Mother.

"She's not home," I said, "She's at work."

"When will she come home?"

"A few minutes after five," I answered.

"Do you have a pencil and a sheet of paper? I'd like to leave a note for your mother," said the tall one.

I invited them in and began rummaging through the papers and boxes on the dining-room table—we always ate in the kitchen. I found a writing pad under a mound of laundry waiting for ironing and a pencil beneath a heap of newspapers. To clear a place for the tall one to write, I pushed aside a heap of brown paper I used for drawing pictures.

The short one took the pencil and wrote the note. "Give this to your Mother," she said.

When they left, the tall one actually patted me on the head.

An hour later mother arrived home with a big smile on her face and a brown-paper bag under one arm. "Stopped at the butcher on the way home to buy a piece of brisket for the weekend. He threw in a large soup bone."

I handed her the note. She read it, recognized her own note paper, and glanced toward the heaped-up table. Her smile disappeared and she roared, "You didn't let them in here did you? With the house in such a mess?"

I just sputtered, but her smile returned as she reread the note. "They want me to come to a meeting at their church. For old times sake—I attended there when I first came to Canada. They'll pick me up by car next Friday evening."

The Friday came and Mother left in a car driven by the short, fat woman. Fred and I felt deserted. With Mom at work during the days we didn't want strangers taking her away in an evening. Mother had rented two rooms of the house to a soldier's wife, Bertha, and her two kids, so we usually had someone else in the house, although we saw them only when they came through to use the bathroom.

On Saturday morning Fred and I rolled out of bed ahead of Mother. Fred, still in his pyjamas, wandered into the living room and saw a large mound on the floor covered by blankets. "What the heck is this?" he said, kicking the mound with his bare foot.

"Yeoow!" he yelled, falling back onto the sofa, and gripping a stubbed toe.

I grabbed the blankets and pulled them free, revealing a great heap of groceries: tins of soup and vegetables, boxes of breakfast food, bags of potatoes, sugar, and flour, and lots of things I didn't even recognize. I did recognize the large pail of honey sitting right where Fred had aimed his kick.

"What's all the noise?" demanded Mother as she entered the room still tying the cord of her bathrobe.

"What, what's all this?" asked Fred still rubbing his toe.

Mother frowned and said, "You know what it is Fred. My old friends had a grocery shower for me last night."

I looked at the grocery pile, but they didn't look wet to me. "Why the heck should I know?" demanded Fred.

Mother turned to face Fred, "Because you got up at midnight and helped carry them in from the car! And quit saying *heck*."

"I helped carry them in?"

"You did. You must have done it without waking up."

Fred, still nursing his toe, said, "Why did you cover them?"

"Actually, you covered them Fred. We did it so Bertha and the kids wouldn't see everything. It's nobody's business if people want to help us by giving us things. Now let's cover them again before they start traipsing through to the toilet."

While Mom and Fred replaced the blankets, I scooped up a tin of Rogers Golden Syrup and headed to the kitchen. Glancing back at Fred, I wondered, "How could anyone carry all that stuff, and not remember it? What kind of screwball do I have for a brother?"

Cub Scouts

Socially, I felt a little awkward in school. I'd arrived to start grade four a year older than my classmates. Then I discovered, according to Ontario school policy, the brighter kids had skipped from third grade to fifth, leaving the less-scholastic in grade four. I resented being one and two years behind others of my age. Although I moved quickly to the top of the class, I developed no friends at school.

For the most part I remained a loner—though not nearly so much as Fred. I looked for something to fill the gap and found it—radio. Somewhere Mother had scraped up enough money to buy an old radio with a gothic speaker grill and a wire antenna that ran outside through a window. It plugged into the power, unlike the battery radio we had on the farm. I soon discovered *Jack Armstrong—the All-American Boy*, *Captain Midnight*, and other kids' programmes to fill in between school and supper time. Indeed, I became a radio junkie—an addiction that has remained.

Patsy lived directly across the street from us. She and her fiancé led the 27th troop of Wolf Cubs at a church a few blocks down Wellington Rd. "Stan, should attend Cubs," she told Mother.

"We don't have any money for a uniform," Mother argued.

"He doesn't need one right away. When he does, we can find a way to get him one."

Patsy convinced Mother, and I reluctantly attended. To my surprise, I enjoyed myself and began to develop a circle of friends. Soon Cubs became the centre of my life, even more important than school and Sunday school—almost as important as the radio!

Maybe I could stay in Ontario after all!

Fred never attended cubs or scouts or made new friends. He just wanted to go back to Alberta.

Christmas in the City

We quickly adapted to Mother leaving us in charge when she headed for work before school began and returned an hour after school ended. We watched for the iceman and opened the door so he could lug the huge block to the wooden icebox in the kitchen. When the route man from the bakery arrived, we'd pay him eleven cents for each loaf and smile shyly when he, with a conspiratorial wink, gave us an extra day-old loaf or package of buns. Some days we'd run out to his wagon to greet and rub the nose of his friendly horse. We'd watch in awe when the horse started without command and stopped at the next customer's house without a word from the driver. We had never seen farm horses show such intelligence—well, maybe Old Dick.

On Thursdays or Fridays Fred and I took over the task of walking four blocks to the meat market to pick up the brisket for the weekend. The friendly butcher would weigh the roast carefully and then include something extra before wrapping it in waxed paper. It seems the whole community had taken an interest in the hard-working mother and her two well-behaved, shy farm boys.

Even before Christmas arrived, I had adapted to my new surroundings. The neighbours got rid of the dog. I no longer walked down the street staring at the huge trees. I had ceased standing at the roadside gaping at the multitudes of cars, trucks, and buses. By the time snow fell, I had adjusted to a large school with only one grade in each room—and only three blocks from home!

On Saturday, about a week before Christmas, Fred, with four quarters stuffed in his mitt and me in tow, headed down Wellington and across the bridge. First we stopped at the barbershop and got hair cuts—two of the quarters gone. We crossed the busy street, ducking expertly between buses and cars (kids learn fast), and began our search for a Christmas tree. We picked one for 40 cents, leaving ten to return to Mother.

Back home, we decorated the scrawny tree with the same ornaments we had used on the farm and listened to Christmas carols on the old radio. A pile of gifts grew under the tree, more than we'd ever seen before, thanks to Aunt Elsie and Uncle Sam. This would be the greatest Christmas ever.

But when the magic day finally arrived, Fred and I, dispirited and pale, dressed in pyjamas, and wrapped in blankets, sat on the floor before the tree. Our necks and jaws had become swollen.

"Mom," I whined, "why did we get the mumps for Christmas?"

I get wheels

As my birthday approached the next June, Mother warned me not to expect a large gift.

"Yeah," I said, "With my luck, I'll likely get chicken pox or measles!"

I didn't get either. Imagine my joy when Aunt Elsie and Uncle Sam delivered a new coaster wagon with my name on it! Although a little old for a wagon, it soon became a major part of my life—I had never had such a wonderful thing that was mine alone. I didn't even have to share it with Fred. "Wagons are for little kids," he sneered.

Joy, who had returned home, loved it. I pulled or pushed her around the neighbourhood and often went to the local shops for Mom. I'd race along the sidewalks with my right knee in the wagon and my left leg providing the motive force—sometimes with Joy sitting in the back corner, squealing with excitement.

Every Saturday throughout that summer I made a very special trip. Alone I'd race along Grand Avenue with a pile of books bouncing along in the wagon and a library card in my pocket. Yes, I had discovered the library. I brought home books on dinosaurs, airplanes, ships, insects, and dogs. I read boys' adventure books and travelled the world with explorers, pilots, and pirates. Indeed, the library became almost as important as the radio and cubs.

The wee train

Long before we moved to Ontario, Mother had told us about a marvellous, miniature, live-steam engine that pulled a train around a track in London's Springbank Park. She had shown us a picture of the train and another with her standing beside Mr. and Mrs. Kennedy, the folks who operated it. She had known the Kennedys since her earliest days in London.

We went to see it on a happy, sunny Saturday. Mother got tickets from Mrs. Kennedy and we climbed into the car behind the engine. I watched in wonder as the engine puffed and wheezed, then accelerated to its normal running speed—about ten or fifteen miles per hour. I didn't look at the scenery going by or pay attention to the running children or waving adults.

My eyes stayed glued to the engine and the heroic man seated on the tender. He wore regulation coveralls and an engineer's peaked cap. An oily rag fluttered from his pocket. One hand worked a throttle protruding from the tiny cab, the other pulled on the cable attached to the whistle. When anyone approached the track, he blew two long and two short blasts. I had seen lots of real steamers, had crossed the country behind one, but this became a memorable event. The little train from the sepia photographs stored in Mother's shoe box had come to life.

After the initial trip, we stood near the tiny platform while others made the short journey. I positioned myself near the spot where the engine stopped and watched in awe as Mr. Kennedy, after each trip, carefully inspected the locomotive, an oil can in one hand and a rag in the other. Before pulling away he opened the door on the miniature fire box and shovelled in coal, inspected the gauges, then in answer to a yell of "all aboard" he opened the throttle. For a few steps he ran beside the engine pushing it to help it get under way, then jumped aboard and chugged off in a cloud of smoke, ash, and steam.

Mother noticed my wonder and said, "Would you like to meet Mr. Kennedy." Without waiting for an answer she pushed me forward so we stood near the place where the engine would stop. The engine pulled in with a squeak of brakes and a hiss of steam.

Mother stepped forward and said, "Mr. Kennedy, this is my second son. He likes your engine."

The engineer answered, "A fine-looking lad." Then he turned to me and asked, "Would you like a ride?"

"I've had one, thank you," I said pointing to the car behind the engine.

"No, I mean with me—up here," he explained, motioning to the tender.

I wasted no time climbing aboard. As we rode, he explained the various controls and said, "Blow the whistle. Two longs and two shorts. That's the railroad signal to warn people to stay off the tracks."

I pulled at the cable and the engine answered with a blast of steam and a shrill voice exactly like you'd expect from a baby engine. Minutes later we arrived back at the platform. Intoxicated with the experience, I leaped from the tender and raced toward Mother.

"Just a moment lad," Mr. Kennedy called after me.

I turned back confused. He placed his hand on my shoulder, looked me in the eye, and said, "You forgot to thank me for the ride."

Deflated, I apologized and thanked him. The edge had gone off my day, but I had learned a valuable lesson.

Alberta visit

The summer after our return to Ontario, Mother, borrowed money from a finance company and took us all to Alberta by bus. She felt it very important that we all visit Pop. We rode right through, changing buses in key cities along the route: Detroit, Chicago, Winnipeg and Calgary.

The drivers allowed people going the greatest distance to board first, so Fred and I almost always got a front seat beside or behind the driver. The tunnel between Windsor and Detroit thrilled us. The first night out, we rode in style around Chicago's lake shore with the lights of skyscrapers reflecting on the water and the driver pointing out landmarks. We raced trains across western Minnesota with the bus speedometer steady at 80 miles per hour and the train slowly dropping behind.

We went straight to Ponoka to visit Pop, but found him confused and unable to communicate. Within a week, and without going to Gawain, we headed home by the same tedious route—Mother had to get back to work to pay off the finance company.

In Detroit Joy and I went for a walk, leaving Mother half dozing on a bench in the depot. Our night-and-day travelling had caused all of us to lose track of time. Joy and I walked three blocks from the bus station, took a right turn, walked two more blocks, and turned right again. I planned to walk in a square, ending back at the depot. We saw no other pedestrians and very few cars. Then a tall figure emerged from the shadows and strode purposefully toward us.

"What are you kids doing here at two in the morning?" a policeman demanded.

I felt no fear; Mother had told us again and again, if you get into trouble, find a policeman. We had no trouble, but the policeman had found us. "Just going for a walk," I answered.

"Where do you live?" he demanded in a voice I thought decidedly unfriendly.

"London, Ontario."

"Well how did you get here?"

"From the bus station." I said. "Mother is at the bus station."

"Ha, where is the bus station?"

That bothered me. Shouldn't a policeman know where to find the station? I pointed along the street and said, "Two blocks down there."

"You are lost. It's this way. Let's get you back there," he said, starting off briskly at right angles to my proposed route. I followed reluctantly.

The officer did know the station's whereabouts. As we entered, he ordered, "Point out your mother."

"There," I said, pointing to a drowsy woman slumped on a bench.

"Are these your children, ma'am?"

Mother nodded.

"Please keep them in your sight. It's not safe in this city in the middle of the night," he said and walked briskly away.

Now fully awake, Mother warned us against further nocturnal wanderings. Not that it mattered; five hours later we entered the relative safety of our own house in London.

Scouts

The following summer I moved from Cubs to Scouts. One day each week I proudly donned the uniform and headed down the street to the church. A gothic archway stood over a heavy wooden door giving entrance to companionship, adventure, and knowledge. Even though I had now spent two years in the big city, I still had many new things to learn. I knew about farming, tracking wild animals, and fending off blizzards and dust storms, but the Scouts could teach me more about city life, living on crowded turf, and decision-making—and about growing up.

One Saturday we all gathered at the home of our Scout leader—a man I idolized. His son Bob acted like a big brother to the whole troop. Ill at ease in surroundings different from the church basement and in a social climate free from the formal and tightly controlled meetings, I retreated to a corner to watch the action.

Bob attempted to draw me out. "You haven't got anything to drink. Come with me," he said. I followed him to the refrigerator.

Pulling open the door he said, "Take whatever kind you want."

I saw shelves filled with an array of bottles—orange, green, brown, and white. I froze. I rarely drank pop. Our one-parent household couldn't afford such extravagance. Bob rattled off a list of brands, but they meant nothing to me. "What kind do you like?" he asked.

"I d'no," I responded without moving. I felt that I faced one of the biggest decisions of my life. I wanted the same kind the other kids had, but I couldn't see their choice from my crouching position in front of the fridge. Twelve-year-old kids, almost by definition, want what their peers have.

"Just take one," Bob pleaded.

I had a sudden brainstorm: "I'll shut my eyes and take the first one my hand touches." Covering my eyes with one hand and reaching out with the other, I grasped a bottle.

"You really don't want that one," said Bob.

"This is okay," I said, getting up. I wanted to get away.

"No, take this one," said Bob, picking an orange bottle from the lowest shelf.

I grabbed it and sped back to my corner. Tucked away by myself drinking my Orange Crush, I puzzled over Bob's strange action. Then as the troop filed out of the basement, I held back so I could peek into the fridge. I saw what I hadn't seen the first time. On the brown bottle I read the word "beer."

I get shot

We enjoyed the old house and property on Wellington Road. The long yard fell away at the back into a river lowland that had served as a dump. Fred and I spent hours poking through other people's trash. If we crossed the dump we could explore the banks of the south branch of the Thames River—to a small degree it replaced our beloved coulee. We planted a garden, but with limited success—Mother had little time to work it or make sure we did.

The house itself proved an ongoing adventure. The previous owner had left many interesting things behind. We found old books and magazines moulding in the basement and attic. The wind-up phonograph came with dozens of ten- and twelve-inch disks. I played one record about a shipwreck over and over until it nearly drove the rest of the family crazy.

Back during our first year in the house, Fred had become a real handyman. He had repaired broken windows and plastered a portion of the dining room wall that had collapsed—although, when finished, it looked like the surface of the coulee pond on a windy day. A lean-to workshop at the rear of the house, still holding a collection of ancient tools, encouraged him to tackle jobs or experiments beyond his ability or knowledge.

By our third year in the house, Fred had grown big enough to take a part-time job working for a large commercial laundry. This curtailed most of his work around the house but opened up other possibilities.

He found a .303 rifle shell in the pocket of an army uniform sent in for washing, kept it, and brought it home—the shell, not the uniform. Thinking it would make a great firecracker, and having a keen interest in firearms, he decided to perform an experiment. He placed the shell in the workshop's vise. Then he leaned a plank against the vise, ducked down low, and prepared to hit the blunt end of the shell with a hammer. He thought the plank would protect him from the resulting explosion. Sensing danger, I ran outside to watch through the window, forgetting it had one pane missing—Fred had not repaired it during his maintenance phase.

The force of the explosion threw me backwards as though I had received a punch on the forehead—but I felt no pain. When I ran back inside and peered through the blue haze, I could see Fred still crouched down, but now with his hands covering his ears.

"Fred, are you okay?" I yelled.

"Yeah, I'm all right. It just . . . sort of . . . stunned me."

He stood up, slowly turned toward me, and blurted, "Oh my gosh, you're all bloody!"

I put my hand to my face and pulled it away dripping blood. We rushed into the house where I washed at the bathroom basin. Fred gave me a piece of cotton wool to hold over the wound just an inch over my right eye where—as I later learned—a small, twisted piece of shell casing had entered. Then the two of us hurried across the street for further help. Patsy, our neighbour and my former cub leader, simply stuck a band-aid over the injury and sent us home. She didn't believe Fred had shot me.

When I displayed my band-aid at school the next day, the teachers and kids didn't believe it either. The following day when I asked people to touch my forehead to feel the object buried against the bone, they still didn't believe I'd been shot.

When people asked Fred about it, he refused to admit a thing!

A startling announcement

About a month before I finished sixth grade, Mother made an announcement that knocked me for an emotional loop. "We're going back to the farm."

She held a letter in her hand from the office of the public administrator in Alberta. Mother had written to him proposing that we return to the farm and, when Fred turned 16, we would lease our land from the public administrator and Fred would farm it. The administrator had written, accepting Mother's proposal.

"Fred isn't 16," I argued.

"No, but it will give us a year to organize—to get equipment and stock."

I began to tremble. "I'll have to leave scouts. And my friends. And Tecumseh school. And this house."

Mother responded, "But you will go back to your old school,

your old home, and your old friends. And we will get our farm back."

I soon realized Mother had been planning this with Fred for months without telling me or Joy—Fred hated Ontario and had decided to return to Alberta when he turned 16 whether we did or not. So I gave up; no one argued with Mother. In fact, as the weeks slipped by, I realized, I didn't want to argue—I began to warm to the idea of returning to Gawain. We'd get horses and a tractor and machinery and soon a car of our own—and the coulee.

The weeks after school ended, found us in a frenzy of activity. Mother listed the house for sale and sold it for $3,200—double what she had paid. She put up posters advertising our household goods and sold almost everything. Fred bought lumber and built boxes and crates for the furniture and other items we planned to take.

Right in the middle of all this Fred became ill—not with the flu or anything like that. He just got tired, as though he had worked too hard at building the crates. Mother remembered Fred's difficult birth. She also recalled that Fred used to turn blue as a baby. Through a contact at the Medical Arts Building where she had recently worked, she arranged for him to see a heart specialist.

The results of the examination staggered all of us—even me. "Fred has a serious heart malfunction. He has a hole between the ventricles of his heart. We can do nothing for him. He should never work hard. If he takes it easy he could live to 60. If he insists on working hard, he will die by the time he reaches 30."

Mother looked grim when she returned home. She sat on the edge of one of Fred's crates and said, "It's too late to change our minds. Fred wants to go anyway. We will have a year or two to see if he can run the farm."

In mid July, we boarded a transcontinental train and headed back to Alberta. Aunt Elsie and Uncle Sam saw us off. They had an added interest; their number three son, Peter, in his late teens, had decided to go with us to work on a farm for the summer.

Section Three: Back to the Land

> Your sons and daughters will prophesy,
> your old men will dream dreams,
> your young men will see visions . . .

Chapter 7

Return Trip

Stop the train!

The train snaked its way out of southern Ontario and into the northland. In a sense we replayed the trip of three years earlier but in reverse. Again I stood between cars at the open window awestruck by the beauty of woods, lakes, and rocks. As before we carried our food with us, but we dashed off at longer stops to buy bread, butter, milk, and tomatoes.

When the train pulled out of the town of Foleyet after a 20 minute stop, we couldn't find Fred or Peter. Mother had sent them for milk. "Stan," Mother pleaded, "Search the train, see if they got on the last car."

I searched every coach on the train without success. Now distraught, Mother appealed for help. The conductor, shrugged his shoulders, "It happens all the time. Kids get off, lose track of time, and miss the train. I'll wire Foleyet from the next station, make sure they're there, and then we can plan something."

Mother sat upright staring out the window, but often with her eyes closed—praying I think. After the next stop, the conductor returned. "The lost boys are okay. They'll get on tomorrow's train. You can wait a day for them in Winnipeg, then continue on."

We did just that. But we really didn't enjoy sleeping overnight on the benches in the Winnipeg station.

New beginnings

We pulled the boards off the windows of the old clapboard house, moved the outhouse to a new site, dropped a bucket into the well, and took up residence. We planned to spend the summer of our return just getting ready for our future farm careers—well, for Fred's future career, because I had grave doubts about ever becoming a farmer. Fred couldn't seriously begin farming until he turned 16 and quit school, but he sure got involved, planning and dreaming with Mom. So after we got the house livable, Mother began buying things.

First she thought of transportation. In Alberta that hadn't changed much in three years, so we knew what we had to look forward to. In springtime roads turned to gumbo, slowing most traffic. In summer the sun baked the dirt tracks rock hard. Then as long as the rain stayed away, even a bicycle could get through. In winter we could expect unplowed snow to block every sideroad. Kids still travelled to school year-round in horse-drawn vans. We lived three and a half miles from town so needed dependable transportation of some sort. Mother took a serious look at a 1926 Ford Model-T but, with her unable to drive and Fred and I too young for licences, she set aside that idea. We bought a team and what our neighbours called a democrat—a true go-anywhere vehicle. If you have never heard of a democrat, picture the buckboard of western films.

Mom, with a lot of help from Fred, bought Daisy, a sorrel trained to saddle and harness. Daisy, along with an old cavalry saddle, became Fred's property. Mom also purchased Queenie to team with Daisy in the democrat. Cousin Peter, with a pink comb holding his long hair in place, rode docile old Queenie. Seeing him at a distance, the neighbours wondered about this strange person from the east—the young fellow who rode with what looked like a pink ribbon in his hair.

For me she bought Tony, my first and only saddle pony. Unable to buy a saddle, I rode bareback. On my first ride, Tony chose to race Daisy back to the barn. He refused to answer my orders, pleadings, or prayers to stop. I kicked off my rubber boots, curled my toes into his armpits, wrapped one hand in his mane, and hung on for dear life. He headed straight for the open barn door; if he entered, I could picture myself splattered across the end wall of the barn!

Tony stopped short of killing me. In fact he stopped with such suddenness that I landed on the ground beneath him with my feet tangled in the reins. Then he waited quietly while I untangled myself and crawled out from between his legs. He didn't laugh out loud, but I saw a twinkle in his eye. I never had much confidence in my horsemanship; that incident further damaged my self image.

Meanwhile on the adjacent farm, my half-brother Willie heard of our antics and felt dismay. He owned and trained race horses and had hoped we would carry on the family tradition and ride for him. Fred showed some ability, but had grown too big to become a jockey. And in Willie's expert opinion, I didn't have a hope as a horseman.

Right on, Willie. I eventually sold Tony and bought a bicycle.

Mother also bought two cows—a frisky young Holstein named Lulu and an elderly, red cow of unknown ancestry. I milked the red cow—we called her Grannie. It proved a simple task. I'd push the pail under her, touch her teats and the milk flowed automatically, half filling the pail. In a few minutes my unskilled hands easily completed the task. Fred had a totally different experience; he had to work for every drop of milk. About every third day Lulu kicked Fred off the stool and into the gutter. Fred responded by breaking the stool over Lulu's back. He wasted a lot of time building new stools until he struck upon using a block of wood sawn from a big poplar tree. Lucky for Lulu, he didn't dare hit her with such a dangerous weapon.

Each morning after milking we'd release the cows into the coulee; at night they'd return, following the old cattle paths through the buckbrush.

We also filled up the henhouse with Barred Rocks and penned off part of the machine shed for White Holland turkeys. I got along well with chickens and soon had a few pets who ran to me at feeding time.

Prior to our hiatus in Ontario, Fred had always killed the chickens. But now I'd turned 13 and Mother passed the task to me. I too-clearly remember my first episode of chicken killing. I held the chicken in one hand and the axe in the other, coaxing it to place its head on the chopping block. The moment I raised the axe to strike, the chicken lifted its head, looked at me, and said in body language, "What's up?"

It took a dozen tries before the chicken finally lowered its guard and lost its head. The horror didn't end there; the headless chicken flopped around the yard squirting blood while it reluctantly died. I later learned to slip an anchored noose of twine over a chicken's head, pull it taut with the bird's neck on the block, wield the axe, and turn my back.

At this point in my life, I positively hated chickens—especially when one of my pets arrived at the execution block.

We got through the winter, riding the school van, milking cows, doing chores, and dreaming—well, Fred and Mom dreamed, I thought of everything but farming. Although we poured over tractor and machinery brochures, I developed a keener interest in airplanes and cars.

Fred and I did agree on one thing. We resumed our love-affair with the coulee. Fred trapped and shot and tracked animals. For the most part I just tagged along or spent quiet times observing wildlife. Fred liked to do more than observe. Armed with a .22 and mounted on Daisy, Fred would chase and occasionally shoot coyotes.

Fred also had important things to do. The fences had suffered from years of neglect, so he made them first priority. Now that we had our own cattle, we needed to ensure that they never broke through fences and got into neighbours' crops. On the less-extreme winter weekends, Fred saddled up Daisy and went in search of trees suitable for fence posts. When he found those he deemed appropriate, he cut them down, trimmed them, and left them piled in convenient places. When he had prepared about 50 posts, he harnessed Daisy and towed the readied posts across the snowy fields to the barnyard. They would become spring's first major project.

Happy birthday Canada

Back in Gawain Consolidated School, I had major adjustments to make. Those of us in the seventh grade shared the classroom and teacher with the eighth and ninth grades. I found myself behind in arithmetic but ahead in most other ways. It took the whole school year to adjust, reestablish old friendships, and once again become a westerner.

Having travelled and seen more of Canada than either classmates or teacher, I became a resident expert. No doubt the recognition boosted my ego and helped fix the time securely in my mind. My storytelling skills even resurfaced with my return to Gawain and my improved self-image.

As the end of the school year approached, the teacher challenged us to honour Canada's upcoming 80th birthday. She talked about the vastness of our great country. I joined in with descriptions of the immense reaches of the prairies, the grassy rolling Saskatchewan plains, the miles of lakes, trees and rocks in northern Ontario, and the great cities and beautiful farms of southern Ontario.

We sang *Oh Canada*, *God Save the King*, and *The Maple Leaf Forever*. I alone had seen real maple leaves, for the leaves of the only maple tree on the prairies, the Manitoba Maple, do not have the characteristic five points. I didn't admit I'd never tasted real maple syrup.

With the war only two years past, we talked about Canada's huge contribution in both world wars. We studied battles where Canadian troops distinguished themselves—Vimy Ridge in the first war and the liberation of Holland in the second. We exulted that Canada had launched and manned the fourth biggest navy during the war. I described how I had seen twin-engine Mosquito fighter-bombers flying over London, Ontario. These machines, produced in a plant near the London airport and sent overseas, had contributed greatly to the war effort.

A Union Jack, a picture of King George VI, and a world map decorated the classroom walls. We studied the map with its predominance of red, and revelled in Canada's historic part in the British Empire and membership in the Commonwealth of Nations. I contributed a pencil sketch of our Governor General, Viscount Alexander of Tunis.

As we talked about Canada's founding peoples, the English and French, we held Wolfe and Montcalm in equal esteem. But the teacher said little about native Canadians. I guess she thought we had learned all about them in the early grades when we built models of Indian and Eskimo villages in a sand table. We felt a sense of unity with our Norwegian, German, Scottish, Polish, and Ukrainian classmates and neighbours. We all liked the Chinese folks who ran the local restaurant.

We didn't set off fireworks for Canada day back then; people at Gawain thought only Americans did that on their national holiday.

I go hunting

For my 14th birthday in June, Fred bought me a box of 50 cartridges and loaned me his .22 calibre Winchester rifle. I donned my rubber boots, headed for the coulee, and began an onslaught on red-wing blackbirds and crows, always making sure no cattle stood in the line of fire.

Tiring of the easy targets, I went looking for a bigger challenge.

Pushing aside the bulrushes, I got a good view of the smallest pond. My feet, already wet from high water in the coulee bottom, sloshed noisily in my rubber boots. I'd hoped to see muskrats, but none appeared on the water's surface. But in the middle of the pond stood a long-legged water bird. I crouched low and watched the beautiful creature blissfully enjoying a siesta; or had it spotted me and decided to seek cover in stillness and silence? I could not remember seeing a bird like it—was it some kind of egret or crane?

After enjoying a few moments as an innocent watcher at the pond, I chose to become an active participant in the struggle for survival. I eased the .22 calibre rifle to my shoulder and took careful aim. The bird calmly awaited its fate. I slipped off the safety catch and gently squeezed the trigger.

Bang! The bullet sped toward the bird, who must have received some forewarning. The creature spread its wings and desperately clawed for safety in the air. "I missed it," I muttered and stood up to watch it gracefully circle the pond.

Then I saw one long leg swinging uselessly beneath the bird's body. It had retracted the other to its normal flying position. I realized I had crippled the creature, likely sentencing it to a slow death. How could it land, or walk, or hunt with a broken leg?

Thinking it better off dead, I fired three shots after it, hoping to bring it down. If you have ever tried to hit a bird in flight with a

.22, you know I could not succeed. Sick at heart, I headed home.

On the way I remembered a similar experience of a few years before. Some kids at school had shown us how to make catapults—we called them sling shots—from forked branches and rubber bands cut from inner tubes. I enjoyed scaring birds by firing stones in their general direction. One day I aimed at a robin, intending to give it a fright. No one would think of hurting a robin, a bird that represents nature's promise of another spring. But, the stone caught the bird in the head and killed it instantly. Struggling with guilt, I told no one, burying the feathered carcass beneath the tree where it fell.

After maiming the water bird, I didn't give up hunting, I even bought an ancient Savage rifle of my own, but I restricted my blood-lusting to creatures I considered predators. During the next months, I dispatched a good number of crows and gophers, but I had lost the desire to kill for killing's sake.

Heart attack!

That spring Fred threw himself into farming tasks. The minute school let out, he began to rebuild the fence lines around the coulee. For a full week he dug post holes with a hand-driven auger, replaced rotten posts, restrung broken wire strands, stretched them with a pulley, and hammered home staples. Each day he came home a little more tired than the day before; each morning he threw himself back into the task, albeit with a little less energy.

On Friday evening he collapsed.

We had a new doctor in town. Dr. Patterson's stint in the army had qualified him to deal with young men—he didn't spare Fred, prescribing complete bed rest for a month. He recommended that Fred give up all thoughts of farming. A thick mist of melancholy settled over the farm.

Fred spent the next week in bed reading Zane Grey and other adventure books. During the second week Mother taught him to knit. When he got tired of knitting he cast about for something to break the boredom.

During the third week he positioned his bed at the window of his second-floor room and shot gophers with his rifle. He aimed at the entrance to the burrow and waited until one popped up its head, then bang. He rarely missed. Soon the whole countryside began talking about his marksmanship.

By the fourth week, he returned to light chores.

"Stan, do you want to farm?" Mother asked me about the middle of the summer, although she must have known the answer.

"No," I answered emphatically.

Mother's dream had once again fallen in fragments about her. Her oldest son could not farm; her youngest would not. She sighed. "I guess it's all my fault. I wanted this to work for Pop's sake. And I wanted to show certain people we could do it—we could win back control of the farm. Maybe we should return to Ontario."

"No way! I'll never go back there," Fred responded.

"Then we'll move to town, into Gawain, while you and Stan finish school."

Father forgive them

During Fred's convalescence a small group of other relatives from Pop's first family dropped in for a visit—people I had not previously met. They had made no contact with Pop or us since his illness. They openly charged that Mother had over-reacted by sending Pop to the mental hospital. They visited him in Ponoka and judged him well—we knew they had arrived on one of Pop's good days. They passed judgment on family members and, when I reacted, they questioned my ability to understand a situation I had lived with for most of my life. They even laughed at Dr. Rich, describing him as a small-town doctor who thought he knew something about mental illness and had ignorantly confined a healthy person.

They chose to ignore protestations of other family members and then returned home never to visit us again. I began to clearly understand the friction between some members of Pop's first family and Mother. They saw her as an interloper trying to get control of the farm. Now I also understood the source of some of the false information that resulted in conflict with the public administrator—I also understood who Mother meant when she talked about showing "certain people."

“They don’t know what they are talking about,” I said in tears to Susan the day after the relatives left.

“No they don’t. They weren’t here and didn’t see for themselves. They didn’t even know Dr. Rich had retired to the practice in Gawain after 30 years as the director of all the mental hospitals in Alberta. Forget about them.”

But I couldn’t forget. I bitterly resented them. They had attacked my mother’s integrity. For weeks intense hatred added to the normal angst felt by most maturing teens. I wanted to fight, to get even for the insults to Mother, but I could find no way to strike back. I wanted to run, but had no place to go. I wanted to curse and throw things, but my training stopped me. Slowly, the worst of the anger subsided, but traces remained for years as an unpleasant tarnish on my nature.

The life of a privateer

A teenager rebounds quickly—especially one who has a new idea. During the time that Fred moped, and knitted, and read in his room, my fertile mind began contemplating our stone boat. “What,” you say, “is a stone boat?”

My father built it years back. He didn’t construct it of stones and he didn’t expect it to float. Some people call it a sledge. Alberta farmers used stone boats to help clear stones from newly-broken prairie.

I looked again at the stone boat. It got very little use. Sometimes a neighbour would borrow it when new stones had worked themselves to the surface of a field. Most of the time it sat in the grass at the corner of the yard, making a good play platform for kids. In our earlier days we would picnic on it or run toys along its flat surface. It made a neat aircraft carrier for our home-made war planes—especially on a windy day when the tall prairie grass swayed and billowed like an angry ocean.

But I had a better idea! As I looked down from the farmyard into the coulee at the two largest ponds, acres in size, an idea struck. In outward silence, but with fervent excitement building within, I studied the old stone boat, then contemplated the closest pond for a few more minutes. I'd do something with it that had never occurred to Pop. I'd turn it into a real boat!

It took me a half hour to pry the contraption free from the ground where it had rested for months. Beneath, where the runners had covered them, a multitude of grubs and bugs scurried for cover as I levered and dragged their roof aside. Somehow I managed to manhandle it 50 yards to the brow of the coulee bank.

Next I pushed the stone boat over the edge and watched it toboggan through the buck brush and sage right down to the coulee bottom. Too late, the wild thought struck me that I should have ridden it down. I ran down the slope and hauled it another 50 yards across prairie grass and reeds to the edge of the pond—it slid more easily on the long grass and wet reeds.

I launched my craft into the water where it floated as beautifully as anything Huck Finn could build. As I pushed off from shore, I thought, "No member of the family, neither Pop nor Fred have ever sailed these waters!"

For the next hour, with the aid of a long pole, I sailed the stone boat on the coulee pond—first as an ancient privateer, then as captain of a great liner. Too soon I heard my mother's powerful mezzo soprano echo across the coulee, "Get that thing out of there before you drown!"

Parents have no imagination!

I harnessed Daisy and, with her willing help, towed my scuttled barque back up the bank to its former resting place.

Prairie sun

"Get your shirt off," Mother ordered. "You need a good healthy tan to help you through the winter."

I glanced at Bert approaching on the road across the coulee bottom. "Bert doesn't take his shirt off," I pointed out.

"Must you always do what your friends do? If Bert stuck his head in the fire, would you do the same? Get your shirt off," Mother ordered.

"Gladys never takes her shirt off," I shot back referring to a blossoming teenager from three farms away.

"That's different, smarty."

Realizing she had no intention of explaining what made it different, and knowing I had pushed Mother far enough, I pulled off my shirt. I considered removing my shirt in the burning hot sun identical to putting my head in the fire. I hated the sun's direct heat, the sunburn, and peeling skin that came from following Mother's orders.

I met Bert on the coulee bank—part way down the slope that erupted with a purple blanket of crocuses under the coaching of spring sunshine. But in mid summer the same sun had matured from gentle oil-lamp to blast-furnace intensity, searing all plant life to deathly brown. We greeted each other, then stood quietly for a moment on the hillside. I broke the silence by saying, "I hate this hot sun."

"Enjoy it while you can. The sun is dying. It will burn out in less than 70 years."

I usually deferred to Bert's superior knowledge. He was Fred's age and just as smart—but that sun statement sounded a little far-fetched. I screwed up my eyes and glanced fleetingly at the orb in question. It looked okay to me, and I could still feel its heat on my bare back. "What are you talking about?"

"I read it in a science magazine," he explained. "Scientists have measured the mass of the sun and computed how long it will take to completely burn. We don't have much time left before it cools and we freeze to death."

"The Bible says, the world will burn, not freeze," I argued.

Bert the unbeliever shrugged, and said, "I prefer to believe in science."

I preferred not to argue and suggested we check out the muskrats in the coulee ponds. The cool shade of the tall rushes appealed to both of us so we raced downhill.

For a few days I worried about the death of the sun, but eventually decided to forget all about it—my distress wouldn't help avert a catastrophe. Later I read the rest of the story concerning that strange scientific projection. The scientists had not understood the atomic nature of the sun's fire and had made their faulty prediction based on the rules of normal combustion.

Since then all of us have learned the danger of excessive sun.

For once I got it right! Science, Mother, and Bert had it all wrong.

Another storm

The weather wouldn't let us leave the farm without having one last shot at us. In the summer of 1947, the dust storms that had devastated the prairies in the 1930s still returned for occasional assaults on central Alberta. An eerie moaning sound warned us of an impending onslaught. Fred heard it first, and despite his recent illness, rushed around the machine shed for a clear view of the western horizon. A huge, black, earth-bound cloud rolled toward our farmstead. Fred pivoted and raced toward the barn, yelling at the top of his voice: "Dust storm! Dust storm!"

All of us sprang into action. While Fred wrestled shut the big barn doors, I sped to the chicken house. Chickens often show more sense then the epithet "bird brain" suggests. Most of them had spotted the approaching terror and scurried into the protection of the hen house. I chased the stragglers in, closed the door, and joined Fred who had now returned to the machine shed. We quickly closed the huge sliding doors, then surveyed the barnyard for loose items that would race before the wind.

Meanwhile, Mother hurried about the house closing windows. She had trained us in quick response, and concerned herself only with her responsibilities, knowing we would take care of ours. Remembering the clothes on the line, she grabbed a basket and did a Dagwood Bumstead run out the back door. For once Fred and I had moved faster, stripped off the laundry, and met her as she came out. Flying arms and legs, scattered shirts and underwear, and peals of laughter added a lighter note to a serious situation.

I grabbed a pillowcase from the teeth of the wind and dashed into the house. Mother turned to me, "Isn't Joy with you? She should be back from visiting Aunt Dolly and Emily."

All of us ran back out of the house into the increasing wind to look along the road as it crossed the coulee bottom and climbed the rise toward the neighbour's place. Through the gathering gloom we saw a tiny wind-buffeted figure running down the slope. She still had a half mile between her and safety. "She'll be terrified," Mother said in matter-of-fact tones.

Before anyone could say another word, and because I knew my ability, I took off at a full run. Fred, older, but heavier, and with his heart problem, should not—indeed could not—run any distance. I, who rarely had a working bicycle or a rideable horse, had learned to run for miles on end.

As the sky grew darker, I dropped over the crest of the hill, raced past the well on the coulee bottom, and entered the road. I caught only glimpses of Joy's tiny form through the driving dust. The wind ripped at my clothes and pushed me toward the ditch. I had visions of it blowing Joy into the ponds at the roadside. She broke into full view as we approached the culvert that drained the muskrat pond. Tears ran down her cheeks, mingling with the prairie dust that coated her face.

I will never forget the look of relief that pushed away fear as she caught my hand. That little adventure, part of living on a prairie farm in the '40s, turned into a magic moment that strengthened forever our relationship.

Chapter 8

Townies

The boarding house

Mother had promised to move to Gawain and move we did. She sold the various animals and equipment we had gathered. With the proceeds and some of the money still left from the house in London, she bought an old house in Gawain. When school opened we had settled in—just over a year after our triumphant return to the farm. Fred, unhappy at the loss of Daisy, nevertheless accepted the inevitable and bigger blow—the loss of his career as a farmer on his father's homestead.

Without the farm animals to provide income, Mother threw our house open to boarders. Her cooking skills soon made it the most popular boarding house in Gawain. Two of our guests worked in retail stores in town. Also, we had two mechanics—one, an older man, Jake, worked at Angus's garage, the other, 19 year-old Hank, worked for the John Deere dealer.

I tried visiting Jake at work, hoping to pick up pointers, but he showed no interest in encouraging me. When I commented that General Motors made both Chevrolet and Pontiac cars, he corrected me. "No, Stan, Chevrolet and Pontiac are different companies. The engines aren't even the same."

To strengthen my argument, I pointed to the *Body by Fisher* insignia on each car.

"That simply means," he said, sighing and shaking his head, "that Fisher made the bodies for both companies."

I decided that I would learn nothing from Jake and shifted my attention to Hank. Hank lived and breathed mechanics and repaired radios as a hobby. Both of these trades excited me. He loaned me books and invited me to join him in the shop when I had free time. But Hank also had another passion—girls.

Suspecting my innocence, he chose to educate me in the facts of life. Fortunately, Noel had recently presented me with a book for boys dealing with the subject, so I had some basic knowledge. Every time I visited Hank in the shop, and I did that often, he would regale me with his conquests and escapades dating back to his 14th year. I did have a keen interest in the subject but, believe it or not, I appreciated more the opportunities to learn about engines and radios!

John Deere

Likeable old Luke Keeler ran the John Deere dealership where Hank worked. Crossing the threshold into the parts department adjacent to the repair shop gave the impression of stepping back to the 1920s. Luke's place remained as one of the few businesses essentially unchanged since Pop's time. The chipped countertop and tattered charts on the wall attested to years of use. I could hear Luke moving about beyond the counter, but found my attention drawn to a piece of green casting on the countertop.

I picked up the piece of painted metal and turned it over in my hands, then looked up to see Luke facing me across the counter. Elderly and overweight, Luke wheezed, pointed a pudgy finger at the casting, and said, "That's part of the first John Deere I ever sold—and it's still running on a farm south of the river."

He stood silently for a moment, looking first at the casting then at me. At last, like a window blind opening, his face lit up and he spoke again: "And I sold it to your dad!"

A tingling sensation ran from the casting through my fingers and up my arms. An effect like a windshield wiper flashed across the room, Luke, and the counter. Luke shed 25 years and the room and the counter gleamed with newness as if reborn. I found myself standing beside Pop—not the aging Pop I knew but a younger man. In my daydream Pop spoke, "I like that new John Deere tractor you have there Luke. If you deliver it to my place next week, I'll give you half the price today and the remainder at the month end."

Luke nodded vigorously, Pop wrote a cheque, and the two shook hands. But before leaving, Pop pulled a folded British magazine from his pocket. "Luke while I'm here, I'd like to ask you something else. Do you think you can get me one of these?"

Luke frowned at a picture in the magazine.

"It's called a rod weeder, Pop explained. "The long rod skims along just beneath the surface of the land, killing the weeds but preserving moisture. I think it would solve many of our farming problems on the prairies."

Luke nodded his head but didn't respond until he finished reading the paragraph beneath the picture. "You really think so, Fred?"

"I certainly do!"

"Then I'll get one for you. In fact I'll order two—if you get one, other farmers in the area will want them. I'll know the price when you come in at the month end."

The windshield-wiper effect swung back through the room and I stood once more before a wheezing, aged, and overweight man behind a battered counter. I placed the casting on the countertop and walked outside, taking the final steps from the 1920s to 1948. Outside, I walked past a new rod weeder awaiting delivery.

Grade eight

Grade eight slipped past. We had a great teacher whom we both loved and hated, Mr. Foster. He had passed retirement age, but rumour said he had an ailing wife and needed to work another year to pay medical bills. He had a room in the teachers' residence and each weekend went back to Edmonton by bus where he lived and had taught for 40 years.

In two weeks Mr. Foster skimmed eighth grade science and then taught us science with the grade nines. He had written the textbook. When the school inspector arrived and questioned him, he said, "The eights have already covered their material, so they're working ahead. They're a particularly clever class."

That year we built electric motors with magnets and wires wound on corks. I began to read every book I could find on auto mechanics and airplanes. I began a collection of glossy aircraft pictures, Stinsons, Pipers, and Aeroncas, and a dozen others. I got them by writing manufacturers in the guise of a farmer seeking an aircraft for transportation. When a salesman offered to visit me and review my requirements, I responded quickly, saying I had lost interest in buying a plane. I didn't want a Piper anyway; I favoured a four-place Stinson Voyager although I had never seen one.

I avoided sports that year as I had done every year. Apparently the design quirk in my system that made me left-handed and unable to carry a tune also limited my skills as an athlete. I liked story-telling, so maybe I could become an actor. I auditioned for and got a key part in the school Christmas concert.

When the big night arrived and the town hall bulged with people, I prepared to make a name for myself. With the other performers, I entered the stage from the front by a short flight of temporary stairs and ducked behind the curtain. An upright piano hid our entrance from the audience.

Not seeing the jerry-rigged electric cables that fed the footlights, I tripped over them and, amid a shower of electrical sparks, plunged the house into darkness. My fellow cast members and I stood in the dark while the local handyman worked on the wires and fuses. Fortunately, my classmates saw it all as humour and fired good-natured barbs my way.

The handyman succeeded in part—we finished the concert and our dramatic presentation under dimmed overhead lights and no footlights. The teachers didn't accept my escapade with the same grace as my classmates. One observed, "We should assign Stan something he can handle—maybe knitting lessons—but he'd likely stick someone with the needles."

I get the picture

My 15th birthday arrived with the end of the school year. Financially, things had improved to the point that Mother gave me a new box Brownie camera—a great gift for a boy who avoided sports and lacked the popularity he yearned for. I couldn't remember a better gift since Aunt Elsie and Uncle Sam had given me the wagon. With new camera in hand, I walked down the alley that ran behind our house and exited behind the R.J. Watsons. Because I did various chores for the R.J.'s, I knocked at their door to pick up my daily assignments.

Mrs. R.J. threw open the door and berated me in language unbecoming of a pillar of the church. In the excitement of my birthday and new camera, I had forgotten to refill her wood box. Well, up until then I had been popular with the old ladies in town. Phooey, when I'm old enough, maybe I'll move back to Ontario.

Alone with a girl

We still had our houseful of boarders. One day Mother planned a trip to Ponoka to see Pop. She hired Gladys for the day to keep an eye on the house and begin the evening meal for the boarders. At breakfast she said to the boarders, "I'll get home about five."

As Hank left for work, he whispered to me. "I'm going to take the afternoon off and drop by to see Gladys alone. I need a little action."

Shocked by his suggestion, I thought quickly. "She won't be alone, Mom has left some chores for me to do."

Hank leered at me, said, "Well then, good luck," and slipped out the door.

When I realized what he meant, I broke into a cold sweat. Determined to protect Gladys' virtue, but with contrary thoughts spinning in my head, I stayed at home until Mother returned. Gladys and I discussed future plans and dreams and I even helped her with some housework.

Hank said nothing that evening. The following day when I dropped by his shop, he looked straight at me, and said, "Well did you have any luck yesterday?"

I spun around and walked out without a word. Out on the street, I wondered what interpretation he had put on my actions. Then in typical teenage, hormone-driven turmoil, I almost wished he had understood my no-comment reaction as "yes."

I go driving

Throughout that summer I picked up pocket money doing farm work for Noel or Willie. Noel had bought his first tractor, a Ferguson, and actually allowed me to drive it. One Friday he came to the house and said, "I'm leaving the tractor at the garage for repairs. Stan, will you pick it up tonight and drive it to my place. You can stay over and help me Saturday."

Obviously, I said yes! I think I yelled yes. I had never driven the tractor without Noel nearby, and I had never driven on the road. That evening with the headlights on, I roared through the darkness—well, it felt like 50 miles per hour, although I don't suppose I got over 15. We spent the next morning tidying up along fence rows—I got to drive the tractor while Noel tossed old fence posts and litter into a trailer.

That afternoon Noel hitched his driving team to the wagon, jumped in, picked up the reins, and headed down the farm lane on our way back to Gawain. His team always moved at a fast trot. The wagon, riding on car axles and wheels, rolled along easily.

Then the unbelievable happened. Noel turned to me and said, "Stan lad, take the reins. If they want to run all the way, let them. They've been cooped up and need exercise."

I reacted in disbelief! Yesterday he had let me drive his tractor on the road—today he offered me the reins of the fastest team in the area.

I took the black leather straps and immediately felt a tremendous pull on my arms. I stood, leaning back with both feet braced, and immediately faced a challenge—getting the team safely through the farm gate and onto the dirt road. I pulled on the lines, at the same time yelling much the way Noel would: "Whoa, whoa back you miserable critters."

I omitted some of Noel's usual words; you never know who might hear. We managed the gate and headed down the road. I eased up on the reins, and the speed increased.

As we raced along, I studied the horses. Maude, on the right, seemed fit and muscular, her narrow back steady as her rear legs pumped rhythmically like the drive rods on a steam locomotive. On the left, Bertha's fat rump wobbled more and her gait seemed less certain. She always stayed a half step behind Maude. Then I realized that the reins to Maude's bridle contained no slack; the tremendous pull on my arms came from her.

Puzzled thoughts crowded my mind: "Teams should be a

matched pair. These two don't look alike, act alike, or work in the same way. Yet I know that no other team in the township can catch them."

I glanced sideways at Noel, almost wishing he would take the lines before my arms pulled from their sockets. He sat on an overturned bucket—his eyes, peeping over the edge of the wagon box, alternated between me and his team. Protected from the wind below the edge of the box, his fingers busied themselves rolling a cigarette.

We quickly overtook a farm tractor towing a manure spreader. I eased the team over to the left of the narrow road, hoping for enough space to slip through. Noel didn't seem to notice as he struck a match on his denim overalls.

As we shot through the slot, I heard the uneven beat of a two-cylinder John Deere. The noise catapulted Maude into a gallop, pulling Bertha with her. Noel feeling the change of pace, popped his head up after lighting his cigarette. "Hold 'em back lad," he yelled, but made no move to grab the lines.

I pulled hard. Maude slowed to a trot and shook her head, emitting a horse-laugh that sounded like a cry of derision aimed at the slow-moving, noisy machine. Bertha let go a wheeze of air that I interpreted as, "Thank God you have slowed down Maude!"

As we approached town, Noel stood up and reached for the reins. I relinquished them with difficulty, for the leather had imbedded itself into my palms. I worked my fingers to regain circulation and wondered if the kids in town would notice that my arms had stretched two inches.

"Well done lad," Noel said. "You handled the team well. You drove like an old-timer."

I yelled my thanks into the wind but thought, "I didn't do the driving. Maude had control all the time. I was just a minor player on a two-horse, one-boy team."

Gosh what fun! Only yesterday, I had driven a tractor on the road at night and now I had driven a spirited team along the same road at twice the speed. Yet somehow I felt trapped between two worlds.

Airborne

I got to know my half-brother Willie much better by doing odd jobs for him. Especially after spending two weeks of backbreaking work burning brush and picking rocks on newly-broken land. Not only did Willie pay me, but he began inviting me to attend various activities around the countryside—places I would never see otherwise. Usually I rode in the back of the '47 Ford pickup with Reggie, while Willie, Jessie, and Orton rode up front—usually Orton drove while undergoing a verbal onslaught from the two back-seat drivers who shared the cab.

One day we went to the fair in Camrose. When I saw an airplane take off from an adjacent field, I hurried to investigate. A homemade sign stated: AIRPLANE RIDES, $5.00. I tried to look casual while waiting for the plane to return even though excitement boiled within me. When the craft approached at right angles to the cow-pasture airfield before turning to land, I got a good look at it—a high wing monoplane with a high tail stabilizer. "A Stinson! It's a Stinson," I said aloud to no one.

I took off running to find Willie; he owed me five dollars.

Back at the plane, the pilot put a young mother and her child in the back seat and signalled me to climb in beside him. We flew over Camrose and the surrounding farmland at 1000 feet at an airspeed of 80 miles per hour. I pointed to the airspeed indicator and said, "How come 80? Won't this plane cruise at 125?"

"Yes, but why waste fuel for a simple joy ride over the town. Where did you learn to read the instruments?"

"Books," I said with a shrug, but thinking, "Heck, anyone can read those things."

The plane landed in a much too-short 15 minutes, but I didn't come down for the rest of the day. On the way home I realized what I had done. Mother and I had discussed my earnings, earmarking that $5.00 for clothes.

On arriving home, I went straight to Mom, confessing that I had spent my clothing money.

She looked up from the ironing board and said, "It's your money. I guess you can do what you like with it."

Right then I made a major decision: one day I'd buy a Stinson!

They're off!

That summer Willie also took me to the races in the town down the tracks from Gawain. He had entered his aging thoroughbred, Flash-K, and his newest acquisition, Jackie's Girl.

On a late summer afternoon, we leaned against the wooden fence and watched the thoroughbreds jockey into position. I could see both of Willie's horses from where I stood. Jackie's Girl moved into a position near the rail while the aging Flash-K languidly shuffled into a much poorer position far from the rail.

"Too bad," said Reggie, "This might be the last race for old Flash-K. At 13 he shouldn't be racing. Dad just brought him along to keep Jackie's Girl company."

A stranger standing nearby overheard and joined our conversation. "Flash-K's a has-been, although at one time there wasn't a horse in Alberta that could beat him. I'm putting my money on Jackie's Girl."

I looked down the track to see Orton on Jackie's Girl. He had ridden Flash-K to many victories in the past and now prepared to use his expertise to guide the new filly to victory. An inexperienced, gangly farm lad clung awkwardly to the back of old Flash-K. Willie never ceased looking for new jockeys.

A lanky farmer stepped up to the rail next to me and sent a spurt of chewing tobacco onto the track. "That your uncle Willie's new colt eh?" he said, looking my way.

"No," I retorted, and stumbled on in awkward teenage fashion, "He is my brother—Willie is my brother, not the horse. The horse is a filly. And he'll win—she'll win."

"Well whatever," the farmer responded. "But your brother's racing days are over until he gets some decent horses. The new filly ain't worth nothin' and old Flash-K's ready for the glue factory. It's a crime to put that old relic on a race track."

Willie and Jessie joined us at the rail in time for them to hear the farmer's comment. Jessie glared at the farmer, but Willie grinned and turned his attention to the track.

"They're off!" crackled the loudspeaker as the field of four-legged contestants thundered past on the dusty track. Jackie's Girl, off to a slow start, began to edge ahead toward the middle of the pack even as they rounded the first turn. Flash-K, the retiree, loped along in the rear, obviously his working days over. As they rounded the second bend Jackie's Girl moved into fourth position and began the battle for third place; Orton low on her neck demonstrated the skill that made him a first-class jockey. Flash-K and the inexperienced rider trailed hopelessly in the rear.

As they rounded the last bend into the final stretch, Jackie's Girl and Orton challenged a big bay for second place. At this point, with victory in sight, the whole Stone clan began to scream and cheer. I cheered and yelled until I became hoarse as I leaped up and down and pounded on the rail. We put on such a display that some people began watching us rather than the horses. As the thundering mass of horseflesh neared the finish line, Jackie's Girl ran neck and neck with the leader.

But a horse race, like so many other events in life, hangs on thin threads of circumstance. A brown form emerged from the pack and hurtled two lengths into the lead, pushing Jackie's Girl back to third place. The screaming Stone family fell silent in stunned disbelief, then exploded again when we identified the miracle winner as Flash-K.

The wily old veteran, ignoring the urging of the young rider on his back, had conserved his energy until the last minute, then for a few seconds performed like a three-year-old. He limped badly as he slowed to a trot, then down to a walk to make his victory pass. I know a teenager's imagination runs wild at times, but I am sure old Flash-K winked at Willie and sneered at the tobacco-chewing farmer.

Grain elevator

By grade nine I had picked up a few new friends: Bert, two years my senior, had dropped out of school and gone to work in the oil fields. I still remained thick with Gord, but I had added Mark, another country kid and the brain of the class. Two town kids, Matt and Roger, joined us to form the Fabulous Five.

With the return of Mr. Foster to Edmonton, Miss Peabody elected to teach the sevens, eights, and nines. She had been around Gawain school for years, but taught the lower grades. She didn't like teenagers and told us so on the first day. For reasons known only to her, she assumed we all had slightly evil intentions. That both embarrassed and pleased us—we chose not to disabuse her.

About a month into school, Matt and I decided to use my camera to do a photo tour of the town. "Let's climb to the top of one of the grain elevators and get some good shots of the town," Matt suggested.

"How do you figure we can get away with that?" I asked.

"We'll ask Mr. McLeod at the Poole elevator. He'll let us climb up the ladder inside the elevator. We can take pictures from the little window at the top."

"Okay," I agreed even though a minute before I hadn't known elevators had ladders. I'd never entered an elevator although I had seen pictures showing how they worked.

We stood for a few minutes looking up at our elevator of choice and talked about them generally. Farmers deliver their grain to an elevator, tipping it through a hatch into a concrete pit built beneath the structure. An endless belt fitted with containers carries the grain from the pit to the top of chutes that disgorge it into bins for storage or cleaning. When boxcars park at the base of the elevator, another set of chutes directs the grain into them.

A typical elevator sits on a base about the size of a small house but rises about five or six stories high. A cupola on top adds another storey to the height and gives the elevator its special shape. We hoped to get to the cupola and look out its window.

Matt and I asked the elevator manager for permission to climb to the cupola by way of internal stairs and ladders. He had recently shut down the mechanism and, knowing us as responsible teenagers, agreed. We climbed to the top, crouched down beside the upper end of the elevating device, and took pictures through the window in the cupola. Dust from the grain coated everything, including us, and filled the air like a thick fog.

Before starting down I pulled a firecracker from my pocket and Matt lit it—we did it in typical teenage fashion without any thought for the consequences. It exploded with a satisfying bang.

With that we climbed down, thanked the manager and went home.

Two days later *The Edmonton Journal* carried a story of an explosion that had completely destroyed a grain elevator in another prairie town. An electrical spark had ignited the grain dust in the air. The story went on to tell how the volatile dust would explode in the presence of fire or spark.

"We did a pretty stupid thing," Matt said the next day.

I agreed. "And if we'd blown it up and killed ourselves, Miss Peabody would have said, See, I was right about at least two members of the Fabulous Five.'"

Miss What's-her-name

Following our return to the farm, our church attendance became sporadic. But when we moved into town, Mother's zeal returned and we never missed a Sunday at the little Mennonite church. Gawain had only two active churches: the Catholic church had a large and faithful following; and the Mennonite church, which acted as the community church for most protestants. It later changed its name to the United Missionary Church.

After moving into town, I became good friends with the Mennonite preacher's son, Josh. He didn't quite fit in with the Fabulous Five, but his arrow-straight morality had a positive influence on me—as did the church generally.

Not that anybody would have thought ill of the good kids that made up the Fabulous Five—well, with the possible exception of Miss Peabody. But they sometimes got into a huddle in the cloakroom and discussed things that would have turned Josh's ears and neck bright red.

One grade eleven girl, I can't even remember her name, particularly attracted the notice of every boy whose hormones had begun flowing. She didn't look all that pretty, but her ample bosom and hips evoked coarse comments—even from some of the moderately straight-laced Fabulous Five. Occasionally one of our group would speculate on the young lady's extra-curricular activities, but I didn't believe them and kept my mouth shut—I rather liked her. Josh and his older brother didn't even know she existed.

Then Matt brought us the story—Cliff told him. Cliff lived on the next farm to Miss What's-her-name. One day after jumping out of the school van and watching its departure, he realized he had left his lunch pail inside. He retrieved his bicycle and followed in hot pursuit, but didn't think he had much chance of catching the van. To his amazement the van turned into the next farm and disappeared behind the barn.

Cliff retrieved his lunch pail and placed it in his carrier, then wondered about the missing van driver and his shapely female passenger. When he heard a giggle from the barn, he crept inside and up the ladder to the hayloft. He later claimed that what he saw almost blinded him! Before descending the ladder, he picked up a piece of female clothing from items carelessly strewn near the top of the ladder.

When we gathered in our huddle to hear the story from Matt, my emotions went into a wild tailspin. I felt every emotion, jealousy of the van driver, heart-pounding desire, disappointment in a girl I had liked, and shame that I let the telling of the event influence me so.

I never shared my feelings of that day with anyone, but I decided I should get control of my thought-life and become more like Josh.

About a month later, Mark and I sat for a moment after class, quietly tossing back and forth a soap company's advertising slogan. One of us managed to put a twist on it of a slightly crude nature—nothing sexy—just something we would never repeat in good company. When we broke out in coarse laughter, Miss Peabody closed in fast, demanding that we share the joke with her.

She delayed us for an hour, but we held firm. No way would we tell her. When she realized she couldn't win, she lectured us, telling how all the teachers in the school knew which boys had smutty or immoral interests—meaning us, of course.

Miss Peabody had it wrong, but we'd never tell her. We left

wondering if she really had concern for our morals, or if she had hoped to hear some salacious adolescent humour.

Maybe we should have shared the hayloft story!

Play ball!

A beautiful fall day under a bright prairie sun did little to ease the tension that knotted my stomach. I stood where experience told me I should never stand—at the plate gripping a bat in sweaty hands. The pitcher seemed more interested in tucking in his shirt, straightening his hat, and impressing the girls than playing softball.

"How," I asked myself, "did I ever let this happen?" A simple series of events had brought me here. The grades eight and nine team had lost a key player to the flu. In desperation they looked around and saw me.

"Stan, come and play. We'll forfeit the game if we go shorthanded. Better to take a full team and lose than forfeit a game," the captain said. I got his implied insult, and still for some inexplicable reason agreed to go.

Now here we were in the bottom half of the ninth with one man on base. The score stood at two to one—for the other team. The pitcher still didn't seem ready; he rolled the ball around in his glove, looking at its miss-shaped form—maybe trying to decide which end to throw first. No use asking for a better ball; we didn't have another.

I thought about the game thus far. My three previous times at bat had produced three rapid outs. With two of those I had retired my team amid catcalls from the bleachers and my teammates. I took a few practice swings while I waited for the pitcher to get on with the execution. He had forgotten the girls and stood scratching himself. If he thought he could psyche me out with his delays he needn't have bothered. Just picking up the bat had done that.

"Play ball," yelled the umpire. The pitcher began his wind-up. Time froze and my life passed by in review. All my softball experience since grade one joined the parade.

The kids played softball during the noon hour at the Gawain consolidated school. The two best players, usually the ones who owned the bats and balls, squared off and began to pick players from those gathered. They always got to me last. Sometimes they treated me like a handicap, saying, "We'll take Stone if you guys'll give us two free runs."

Once they picked me third from last because two girls wanted to play.

I returned to the present when the pitcher checked his wind-up, turned, and fired the ball to first to try to catch our runner. A war nearly started over that one. Our team yelled, "Balk," while theirs retorted, "Your pitcher does it all the time." Why couldn't we just get this over! The noise subsided and the pitcher finally started his wind-up again.

As I stood waiting, I realized it wasn't just softball. Once I tried to play hockey in grade three. No one wanted me then either. It seems that players who skate on the sides of their feet come low in the draft. A teacher stepped in and insisted they let me play. After two or three minutes on the ice a big fight started. Seeing the puck unguarded I trundled down the ice and pushed it into the net. That just made the row worse. Eventually, the teacher calmed the players, declared my goal invalid, and got the game going. One minute later as the opposing team charged our net, a speeding puck struck me on the temple and dropped me to the ice. My heart hurt more than my head; it seemed that neither of the teams nor the teacher wanted me around.

I snapped back to reality as the ball came speeding toward me. Well it didn't really speed. The bump on it made it skip through the air like a stone on water. "Get it over with," I thought. The last words of the poem *Casey at the Bat* echoed through my mind as I began the swing.

The resounding crash of wood against leather stunned me. I stood motionless with a loud ringing in my ears. Then I heard people screaming, "Run! Run! Run!"

I ran. Our team won. For the next week my ears resounded with the greeting, "Home run king." One fortuitous swing had raised me to star status. The next time the gang gathered at the diamond they almost fought over me.

"No," I said, "I'll sit this one out." I knew when to quit.

The wanderlust again

Part way through the ninth grade, Mother shrugged her shoulders and said, "We'll have to move on. There's nothing here for you boys."

Mother had work in mind, not education; although Gawain didn't offer much in the way of educational opportunities either. Mom, who attended school for only five years herself, had little understanding of the value of education. She simply hoped her boys would soon get work to remove from her all the weight that falls on the shoulders of a single parent and sole breadwinner.

I wanted to get a job in a garage and drop out of school when I turned 16; that idea seemed to harmonize perfectly with Mother's philosophy. I argued, "Why can't I get a job here in Gawain? The garages and farm machinery places in town hire mechanics. I've been reading books and I'd make a good mechanic."

"Just look around and see whose kids get jobs in this town. We don't belong to the right crowd; we don't really know the right people," she snapped back.

"But Mother . . ."

"Don't 'but Mother' me. Getting ahead in life depends on who you know, not what you know. And they have garages in Ontario . . . and in British Columbia."

That cynical reaction from Mother shook me up. In fact it opened a large crack in my teenage shell of idealism. But I had got the main message; we'd soon move again.

But then, wasn't that what I really wanted?

Did Mother actually mention British Columbia? Did she want to move to B.C.? I challenged her. "Yes I'm thinking of B.C.—Kelowna to be exact. Two or three families from Gawain have moved there, including my best friend, Margaret. She says there's plenty of work for you boys in Kelowna."

I remembered the Boy Scouts, the beautiful trees, Aunt Elsie and Uncle Sam, the big city, the libraries, and asked, "Why don't we move back to Ontario?"

"Because Fred won't go to Ontario. Although he really wants to stay here, he has agreed to move to Kelowna. And Kelowna is close enough that we can still visit Pop."

An angel unawares

Following Mother's decision to move to Kelowna, she slipped into a depression. I suspected she harboured some uncertainty about the proposed move. For at least one week she ceased singing as she worked and the edge went off her humour. She received a slight boost on Saturday when someone rapped on the back door. Abandoning her bucket and scrub brush in the middle of the kitchen floor, she hurried to answer the knock.

"Hello Harriet," greeted the pastor's wife. "Could I have a moment to speak to you about the ladies missionary society?"

"Yes, do come in," Mother answered. "In fact you just caught me on my knees."

"Wonderful! All of us should spend more time on our knees in prayer."

"I agree with that, but I did have something else in mind," said Mom, laughing and pointing to the bucket and scrub brush.

Fortunately, the pastor's wife had a good sense of humour. But even that moment and the Sunday services didn't pull Mother out of her slump.

On Wednesday she heard and answered a timid rap at the door. On our back steps she found a short older man wearing a dark suit and a long grey overcoat. He carried a black satchel, wore a slouch hat on his head, and sported an Abe Lincoln-style beard. "Can I help you?" Mother asked.

"Good afternoon, Mrs Stone. The lady at the post office told me that you might be able to provide me with a room and board for two nights while I'm in town."

Mother hesitated, "Well . . ."

"I'm Pastor Watts, a preacher. I would like to hold a preaching service in town and need a place to stay."

"Do come in," said Mother. "I'm sure I can find a corner somewhere."

Mom found that corner; she turfed me out of my room! For the rest of that day and the next Pastor Watts brightened up our home—even the boarders liked him. On Thursday morning, he busied himself by arranging to use a school room and putting up handwritten notices of his preaching service. On Thursday afternoon he retreated to my room—his room—to "pray and prepare" as he said.

And Mother had begun singing around the house once more.

That evening Mother, Joy, and I attended the service—along with two elderly women. Pastor Watts showed no signs of discouragement; indeed he preached on overcoming despair. The following morning after breakfast, he said goodbye and walked into light falling snow, carrying the black satchel we now knew held his big Bible and little else.

Ten minutes after he left, I found a small notebook in my room. When I showed it to Mom, she sent me chasing after the preacher. I searched the town, checked in every store, asked at the railway station, the post office, and the restaurant where people bought bus tickets. No one had seen the man. No one had noticed him leave our house. When I couldn't find him, I checked for the notices he had posted for the preaching service. I found none.

Back at the house I shared the results of my search with Mother. She showed no surprise at all. "I felt so discouraged, thinking about moving again. God sent him along just to encourage me. The Bible says some people have entertained angels unawares. I believe we did just that."

We're off

By the end of April, Mother had sold the house to Willie and Jessie, disposed of furniture and many other possessions, and moved to Kelowna with Fred and Joy. She left me with Susan and Eric and family so I could finish the ninth grade. I found myself back riding the school van for the final six weeks of the school year.

"What will you do in Kelowna?" asked Susan.

"Get a job in a garage and get my mechanics papers."

"You should finish grade 12," she said.

"No way. When I leave here, I'm through with school for the rest of my life."

"You'll be sorry one day."

I really meant it when I insisted, "I'll never, never regret that I quit school!"

Mountains

The bus rolled steadily from Calgary toward Banff and the mountains. Gord and I leaned forward in the front seat as the green, rolling foothills filled the broad windshield of the Greyhound. "They're not all that great," Gord said. "No taller than the coulee banks at the Battle River."

The Battle, lying within its coulee or valley, wends its way north and east across the Alberta prairie, passing a few miles from Gawain. Gord and I had visited the River just weeks earlier. With my box Brownie, I had taken some goodbye pictures of part of the world I didn't expect to see again. Gord planned to return after the summer vacation, but I intended to begin a new life with my family in Kelowna, B.C.

I studied the hills ahead and fervently and loudly agreed with Gord in a candid teenage manner. Those mountains ahead didn't impress me in the least. At age 16 both of us had arrived at that plateau in life where we knew 99 percent of everything we would ever know. I knew I'd become a mechanic; I knew I didn't need any more education. I knew I had all I needed to meet any challenge life might toss my way. And now I knew that people had exaggerated the majesty and beauty of the Rockies.

Very soon we rolled into high mountain passes with great ravines falling away below and towering snow-capped peaks reaching high above us. Chagrinned, I glanced around, then said to Gord in tones just loud enough for our fellow passengers to hear, "Well, I guess they are a little higher than the banks of the Battle River."

I didn't know it, but I had many huge mountains and deep valleys ahead—so far in my life journey I had crossed only the foothills.

Epilogue

When I became a man
    I put childish things behind me.

No doubt about it; the foothills of my teens prepared me for the mountains and valleys of adulthood.

When we got to B.C., we found Margaret had given bad advice—Fred and I couldn't find lasting work. We stayed only a few months then returned to Ontario—Fred soon backtracked to Alberta where he worked hard and died in his forties.

After returning to Ontario, Mother appealed directly to Premier Ernest Manning during one of his visits to Ontario. Through his influence, the Public Administrator sold the farm to Brother Willie and gave Mother one third of the proceeds.

Pop died in 1959. Although I rejected farming as a lifestyle, I did manage to emulate him in many other ways: I lived for a time in South Africa; visited India, Australia, and many other places; travelled widely; and became an editor and writer.

In the remainder of her life, Mother moved at least ten times—and I have done better than that!

I got fired by three garages before getting the message, but began the first of four careers as an electronic technician in a radio shop. Rather than rue the day I quit school, I just moved on from there. I never earned a high-school diploma, but I managed to graduate from Radio College of Canada and the University of Waterloo.

That little Mennonite church and my friend Josh must have had a fair amount of influence on me—in my late 20s, I attended Briercrest Bible College and entered the ministry—my second career.

Although it took years, I made a conscious decision to forgive "certain" family members. It changed my life for the better, and family relations improved greatly. I'm sure you noticed the tension between Fred and me that traced way back to the days he insisted my real father still lived in England. We outgrew the animosity and became good friends.

I didn't buy a Stinson, or any other plane—but my youngest son did (I have four sons), and he has promised to teach me to fly.

Flash-K retired without running another race, and I never again played softball.

Oh yes, thinking back to second grade—I learned to live with and overcome problems associated with dyslexia. But as you may have noticed, I have fully regained my passion for storytelling!

FRED STONE FAMILY TREE

Key characters: **Bolded**

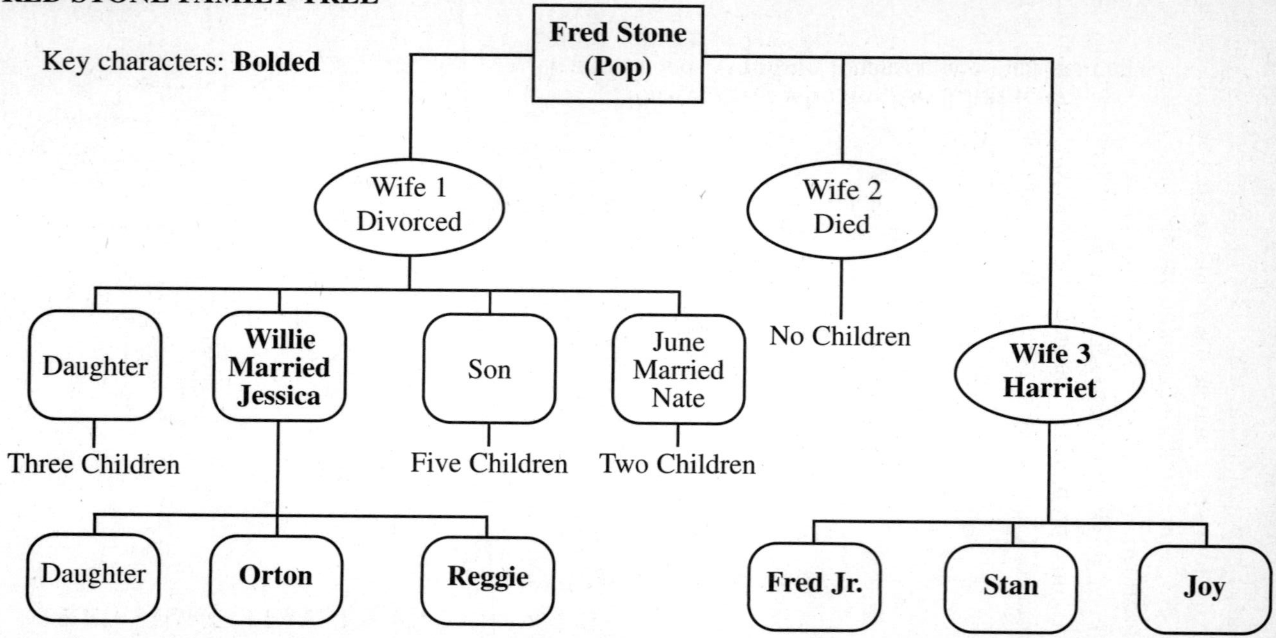

FRED STONE'S FATHER AND SIBLINGS

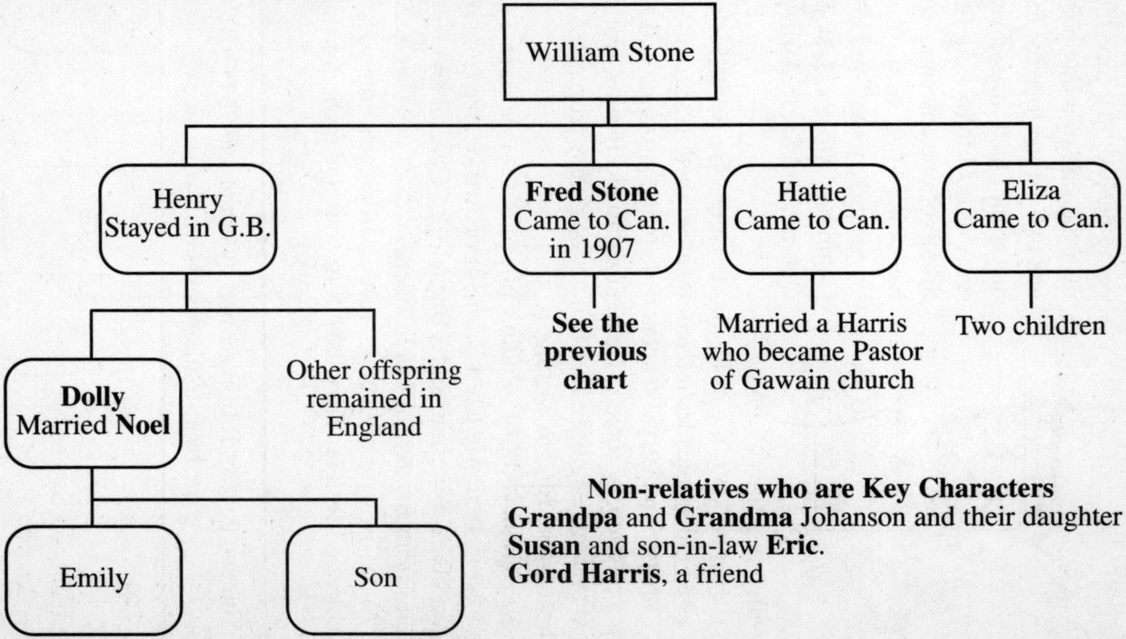

Non-relatives who are Key Characters

Grandpa and **Grandma** Johanson and their daughter **Susan** and son-in-law **Eric**.

Gord Harris, a friend

ABOUT THE AUTHOR

Ray Wiseman's early memory—being pushed up a rope ladder and over the side of a tramp steamer at age two set the tone for his life. He has spent much time travelling, and most of his life looking from the hilltop of one adventure to the beginning of the next. Born in England, Ray has lived in British Columbia, Alberta, Saskatchewan, Ontario, and South Africa. He has travelled in Africa and Asia.

Ray counts writing as his fourth career. He began his working life as an electronics technician, then returned to school to study for the Christian ministry. He spent time in the pastorate and overseas with a missionary society. He returned to electronics, working as a video systems engineer. In 1993, he took early retirement to dedicate more time to writing.

Ray graduated from Radio College of Canada (now RCC Schools) in 1952. He has a Bachelor of Arts degree from the University of Waterloo, and a Bachelor of General and Biblical Studies from Briercrest Bible College.

Anna, his wife of over 45 years, participates enthusiastically in his eclectic lifestyle. They have four sons and eight grandchildren.

You can contact Ray Wiseman by telephone, (519) 787-0178,
or by E-mail at rsw@wordwise.on.ca

If you have trouble getting Ray's books through your local bookstore, you can order them from:

WordWise Associates
12—215 Belsyde Avenue E.
Fergus, ON N1M 1Z4
Canada

A Difficult Passage $16.95

Disciples of Joy. $14.95

The remarkable story of a Hindu priest who became a communist organizer before converting to Christ. Written for Partners International.

Aunt Harri Walks the Line $14.95

A feisty old lady faces the challenges of aging with dignity and humour. Drawn from newspaper columns published over the years.

I Cannot Dream Less $12.95

An Indonesian from a remote island proclaims a message that changes his nation. Written for Partners International.

The above prices are in Canadian funds; for US dollars, use the current exchange rate. If you enclose a cheque with the order, we will cover shipping costs.

Want more information?
Phone: (519) 787-0178
or e-mail: rsw@wordwise.on.ca